Current
CONTROVERSIES

| Cyberterrorism

D1738300

Other Books in the Current Controversies Series

Cyberterrorism

Erica Grove, Book Editor

GREENHAVEN
PUBLISHING

Published in 2022 by Greenhaven Publishing, LLC
353 3rd Avenue, Suite 255, New York, NY 10010

Copyright © 2022 by Greenhaven Publishing, LLC

First Edition

Articles in Greenhaven Publishing anthologies are often edited for length to meet page
requirements. In addition, original titles of these works are changed to clearly present
the main thesis and to explicitly indicate the author's opinion. Every effort is made to
ensure that Greenhaven Publishing accurately reflects the original intent of the authors.
Every effort has been made to trace the owners of the copyrighted material.

Cover image: REDPIXEL.PL/Shutterstock.com

Library of Congress Cataloging-in-Publication Data

Names: Grove, Erica M., editor.
Title: Cyberterrorism / Erica Grove, book editor.
Description: 1 Edition. | New York, NY : Greenhaven Publishing, 2022. |
  Series: Current controversies | Includes bibliographical references and
  index. | Audience: Ages 15+ | Audience: Grades 10–12 | Summary:
  "Anthology of curated articles exploring cyberterrorism and cyber
  attacks used to create chaos and fear. The viewpoints in this resource
  debate the potential damage created by cyberterrorism, how it can be
  prevented, and who is responsible for policing it"— Provided by
  publisher.
Identifiers: LCCN 2021029611 | ISBN 9781534508651 (library binding) | ISBN
  9781534508644 (paperback) | ISBN 9781534508668 (ebook)
Subjects: LCSH: Cyberterrorism—Juvenile literature. | Computer
  crimes—Juvenile literature.
Classification: LCC HV6773.15.C97 C937 2022 | DDC 363.325—dc23
LC record available at https://lccn.loc.gov/2021029611

Manufactured in the United States of America

Website: http://greenhavenpublishing.com

Contents

Chapter 1: Is Cyberterrorism Distinct from Cyberwarfare and Other Cyberattacks?

Fawzia Cassim

This excerpted viewpoint argues that the absence of suitable legal frameworks to address cyberterrorism at national and regional levels, the lack of adequate safeguards, the lack of cybersecurity strategies, and the preoccupation of countries with internal factors have all contributed to the creation of an environment that can be easily infiltrated by cyberterrorists.

Yes: Cyberterrorism Differs from Other Types of Cyberattacks

Laura Mayer Lux

This excerpted viewpoint demonstrates cyberterrorism's relationship to terrorism and to other cybercrimes while clarifying what characteristics set it apart from these crimes. For a cyberattack to be considered cyberterrorism, the "harm principle" must be met.

Donald L. Buresh, PhD, JD

In this excerpted viewpoint, the author argues that, while controversial, digital terrorism is as real a threat as conventional terrorism. As technology advances, however, future cyberattacks will not resemble past attacks.

Rory Carroll

In 2014, a hacker group leaked confidential data from Sony Pictures and threatened terrorist attacks at theaters showing Sony's film *The Interview*, which depicted North Korea in a negative light. The US blamed North Korea and threatened to place the country on the State Department's terrorism sponsorship list.

No: All Forms of Cyberattacks Have the Same Effects, and the Distinctions Between Them Are Arbitrary

Chapter 2: Is Cyberterrorism a Significant Threat?

Yes: Cyberterrorism Has the Potential to Cause Real Damage

grids suggest how such attacks could turn deadly. Unlike with nuclear weapons, there are no international protections against cyberattacks.

Emma Graham-Harrison

ISIS recruits hackers to join its "cyber caliphate," and given the devastation the group has caused through real-world attacks, it is safe to assume that their hackers aim to do similar damage online. Although so far their online activities have been largely limited to creating propaganda, recruiting new members, and hacking for profit, it isn't a stretch to assume that sabotaging physical targets through hacking could be on the agenda.

Dorothy E. Denning

Iran's Islamic Revolutionary Guard Corps, a branch of its military, has been developing cyberattack capabilities for years. It contracts independent hacking groups to carry out the attacks, which makes it even more difficult to attribute them. So far, the attacks have been limited to cyber theft and DDoS attacks on desktop computers and standard commercial servers, but the potential for them to target industrial control systems for physical infrastructure exists.

No: Cyberterrorism Is Not Nearly as Dangerous or Deadly as Real-World Attacks

Irving Lachow and Courtney Richardson

The authors of this excerpted viewpoint argue that although the internet is an important resource for terrorists, cyberterrorist attacks are unlikely. Through examining how terrorists do and do not use the internet, the authors assert that the threat of cyberterrorism has largely been exaggerated.

Gabriel Weimann

At the time of this excerpted viewpoint's publication, the author argued that there had been no recorded incidents of actual cyberterrorist attacks on US public facilities. Though high-profile and costly attacks have occurred within the US since then, this assertion continues to be true. The attacks that have occurred are by individual hackers and insiders seeking to profit, not terrorist organizations.

Chapter 3: Should Governments Be Responsible for Preventing Cyberterrorism?

Yes: Government-Led Cybersecurity Initiatives Have the Best Chance of Being Successful

The Cybersecurity Act of 2012 was introduced to Congress with the intention of protecting the government and various industries from cyberattacks by putting in place required cybersecurity standards. The bill was ultimately voted down in the Senate, but it pointed out the lack of existing legislation to protect Americans from cybersecurity attacks.

No: Private Corporations and Organizations Should Be Responsible for Their Own Cybersecurity

Attacking would-be hackers before they can attack you may only serve to further provoke the hackers. Annoyance and attribution are two legal options for active defense. Private companies and individuals should focus on utilizing and developing these options.

Chapter 4: Is It Possible to Effectively Combat Cyberterrorism and Other Cyberattacks?

Yes: Cyberterrorism and Other Cyberattacks Are Generally Preventable

No: Cyberterrorists and Other Cybercriminals Will Always Have the Upper Hand

Cynthia Brumfield

It is not always possible to determine who is behind a cyberattack. This viewpoint examines how cyber attribution occurs online and the weaknesses in these techniques. Ultimately, the author argues that uncertainty will always be a part of cyber attribution.

Nir Kshetri

In 2016, a hacker group known as the Shadow Brokers successfully attacked the US National Security Agency, one of the most high-profile cybersecurity breaches in the US. Cyberweapons and cyberattack tools have become extremely sophisticated and easier to access, which means more attacks on high-profile military, political, and economic targets around the world are likely.

Foreword

Controversy" is a word that has an undeniably unpleasant connotation. It carries a definite negative charge. Controversy can spoil family gatherings, spread a chill around classroom and campus discussion, inflame public discourse, open raw civic wounds, and lead to the ouster of public officials. We often feel that controversy is almost akin to bad manners, a rude and shocking eruption of that which must not be spoken or thought of in polite, tightly guarded society. To avoid controversy, to quell controversy, is often seen as a public good, a victory for etiquette, perhaps even a moral or ethical imperative.

Yet the studious, deliberate avoidance of controversy is also a whitewashing, a denial, a death threat to democracy. It is a false sterilizing and sanitizing and superficial ordering of the messy, ragged, chaotic, at times ugly processes by which a healthy democracy identifies and confronts challenges, engages in passionate debate about appropriate approaches and solutions, and arrives at something like a consensus and a broadly accepted and supported way forward. Controversy is the megaphone, the speaker's corner, the public square through which the citizenry finds and uses its voice. Controversy is the life's blood of our democracy and absolutely essential to the vibrant health of our society.

Our present age is certainly no stranger to controversy. We are consumed by fierce debates about technology, privacy, political correctness, poverty, violence, crime and policing, guns, immigration, civil and human rights, terrorism, militarism, environmental protection, and gender and racial equality. Loudly competing voices are raised every day, shouting opposing opinions, putting forth competing agendas, and summoning starkly different visions of a utopian or dystopian future. Often these voices attempt to shout the others down; there is precious little listening and considering among the cacophonous din. Yet listening and considering, too, are essential to the health of a democracy. If controversy is democracy's lusty lifeblood, respectful listening and careful thought are its higher faculties, its brain, its conscience.

Current Controversies does not shy away from or attempt to hush the loudly competing voices. It seeks to provide readers with as wide and representative as possible a range of articulate voices on any given controversy of the day, separates each one out to allow it to be heard clearly and fairly, and encourages careful listening to each of these well-crafted, thoughtfully expressed opinions, supplied by some of today's leading academics, thinkers, analysts, politicians, policy makers, economists, activists, change agents, and advocates. Only after listening to a wide range of opinions on an issue, evaluating the strengths and weaknesses of each argument, assessing how well the facts and available evidence mesh with the stated opinions and conclusions, and thoughtfully and critically examining one's own beliefs and conscience can the reader begin to arrive at his or her own conclusions and articulate his or her own stance on the spotlighted controversy.

This process is facilitated and supported in each Current Controversies volume by an introduction and chapter overviews that provide readers with the essential context they need to begin engaging with the spotlighted controversies, with the debates surrounding them, and with their own perhaps shifting or nascent opinions on them. Chapters are organized around several key questions that are answered with diverse opinions representing all points on the political spectrum. In its content, organization, and methodology, readers are encouraged to determine the authors' point of view and purpose, interrogate and analyze the various arguments and their rhetoric and structure, evaluate the arguments' strengths and weaknesses, test their claims against available facts and evidence, judge the validity of the reasoning, and bring into clearer, sharper focus the reader's own beliefs and conclusions and how they may differ from or align with those in the collection or those of classmates.

Research has shown that reading comprehension skills improve dramatically when students are provided with compelling, intriguing, and relevant "discussable" texts. The subject matter of these collections could not be more compelling, intriguing, or urgently relevant to today's students and the world they are poised to inherit. The anthologized articles also provide the basis for stimulating, lively, and passionate classroom debates. Students who are compelled to anticipate objections to their own argument and identify the flaws in those of an opponent read more carefully, think more critically, and steep themselves in relevant context, facts, and information more thoroughly. In short, using discussable text of the kind provided by every single volume in the Current Controversies series encourages close reading, facilitates reading comprehension, fosters research, strengthens critical thinking, and greatly enlivens and energizes classroom discussion and participation. The entire learning process is deepened, extended, and strengthened.

If we are to foster a knowledgeable, responsible, active, and engaged citizenry, we must provide readers with the intellectual, interpretive, and critical-thinking tools and experience necessary to make sense of the world around them and of the all-important debates and arguments that inform it. We must encourage them not to run away from or attempt to quell controversy but to embrace it in a responsible, conscientious, and thoughtful way, to sharpen and strengthen their own informed opinions by listening to and critically analyzing those of others. This series encourages respectful engagement with and analysis of current controversies and competing opinions and fosters a resulting increase in the strength and rigor of one's own opinions and stances. As such, it helps readers assume their rightful place in the public square and provides them with the skills necessary to uphold their awesome responsibility—guaranteeing the continued and future health of a vital, vibrant, and free democracy.

Introduction

> *"While the vast majority of hackers*
> *may be disinclined towards violence,*
> *it would only take a few to turn cyber*
> *terrorism into reality."*
>
> —*Dorothy E. Denning,*
> *American information*
> *security researcher*

Though not the first terrorist attack to occur on US soil, the September 11, 2001, attacks on the United States by the terrorist group Al-Qaeda can be credited for imprinting the threat of terrorism on the public consciousness. Finding ways to prevent such attacks from occurring has been the focus of numerous government agencies, organizations, and legislative proceedings over the past two decades. For instance, some of the notable ways this manifested in the US was with the passage of the Patriot Act in October 2001[1] and the creation of the Department of Homeland Security in March 2003.[2] These have shaped the issues of domestic security, government surveillance, and international relations ever since, and it should come as no surprise that the internet—which in the intervening decades has simply become more sophisticated and omnipresent—is one arena in which the fight against terrorism is taking place.

The potential damage that could be brought about by cyberterrorism became evident during the April 2007 cyberattacks on the websites of Estonia's banks, parliament, news organizations, and ministries. These websites were repeatedly attacked over the course of the month by distributed denial-of-service (DDoS) attacks, which resulted in the jamming and disabling of the websites.[3] Since the cyberattacks followed the removal of a Soviet war memorial, Russia was considered the top suspect. Though the attacks have been labeled as acts of cyberterrorism and cyberwarfare, the fact that the internet could be the location of attacks as sophisticated and harmful as these served as a wakeup call.

Cyberterrorism is a concept that continues to strike fear in governments, corporations, and private citizens. According to a 2021 Gallup poll, 82 percent of Americans surveyed consider cyberterrorism to be a critical threat, placing it at the top of the list of potential threats—above infectious disease and the development of nuclear weapons by North Korea and Iran.[4] However, despite its perception as a critical threat to society, cyberterrorism is not necessarily clearly understood. The definition of cyberterrorism is murky and often contested. As Lee Jarvis and Stuart Macdonald explain in their paper on the issue, the difficulty in defining cyberterrorism can be boiled down to two questions:

> The first is referential: to what does, or should, the term cyberterrorism refer? The second is relational: how is cyberterrorism similar to, and different from, other forms of violence or behaviour? Is it, for instance, a distinctive phenomenon with its own characteristics? Or is it a sub-species of terrorism which itself constitutes a broad and diverse category of violence?[5]

When considering the relational aspects of cyberattacks, many experts agree that in order to qualify as cyberterrorism, the internet must be used to cause "injuries, bloodshed or serious damage, or fear," though "fear" and "serious damage" are largely subjective terms.[6] Some experts extend their definition of cyberterrorism to include not just attacks that are made on the internet but also the use of the internet to support terrorist organizations in activities like recruitment and funding as well. While it is easier to see how cyberattacks can cause fear and damage infrastructure and corporations, real-world harm resulting in injury or loss of life can be difficult to trace back to a cyberattack. At this time, no instances of cyberterrorism resulting in bodily harm have been recorded.[7, 8]

How cyberterrorism is defined differs widely depending on who it is that is providing the definition. According to a relatively broad definition offered by the US Federal Bureau of Investigation (FBI) in the wake of the September 11, 2001, terrorist attacks, cyberterrorism is "the use of cyber tools to shut down critical national infrastructures (such as energy, transportation, or government operations) for the purpose of coercing or intimidating a government or civilian population."[9] However, the issue with this definition is that it could just as easily be applied to cyberwarfare.

This flaw demonstrates one of the criticisms about defining cyberterrorism, which is that it is often a matter of perspective. For instance, by this definition, the 2010 attacks on Iran's Natanz nuclear facilities by the US- and Israeli-created virus Stuxnet would be considered cyberterrorism, but the US government would likely characterize it instead as an act of cyberwarfare that is necessary in dismantling Iran's dangerous nuclear program.[10] Iran, however, would likely take the opposite stance. The earlier example of the 2007 cyberattacks in Estonia similarly demonstrates how intertwined and often interchangeable cyberwarfare and cyberterrorism can be.

The FBI has since come to update its definition to a "premeditated, politically motivated attack against information, computer systems, computer programs and data which results in violence against non-combatant targets by sub-national groups or clandestine agents."[11] With this definition, the FBI has clarified that the attacks need to be made by "sub-national groups or clandestine agents" rather than by nations themselves, but—as with many things on the internet—anonymity is an issue in defining cyberterrorism as well. Often it can be difficult for authorities to determine who is responsible for a cyberattack and even more difficult to verify if they are acting on their own, as part of a terrorist organization, or on behalf of a country in an act of cyberwar.

In rare cases, however, it is possible to both track down the attacker and determine that the cyberattack was intended to have lethal effects. In 2015, Ardit Ferizi, a Kosovan hacker, was detained in Malaysia and charged by the United States Department of Justice (DOJ) with stealing the personal information of US service members.[12] Ferizi gave this data to the terrorist organization ISIS, which then urged its followers to attack these service members. This was the first case in which someone was charged with cyberterrorism in the United States, moving cyberterrorism from the realm of abstraction to reality.

In order to prevent cyberterrorist attacks and ensure cyberterrorists are held accountable, there are several variables to take into consideration. Cyberattacks and suspicious activity need to be traceable to individuals, which is a significant challenge on the internet and a major goal of cybersecurity professionals. Then, determining that a cyberattack falls under the definition of cyberterrorism, rather than cyberwarfare or another form of cyberattack, is necessary for punishing attackers. This makes legislation at the federal and international level an important piece of the puzzle. Since these attacks take place on the internet, the attacker will often be located someplace other than the country under attack, which causes international cooperation to be especially important in addressing cyberterrorism.

Because cyberterrorism is often so difficult to trace, preventing cyberattacks from happening in the first place may be the best option. Cybersecurity experts are exploring different ways to protect private citizens, corporations, and governments from these attacks, and the US government can ensure that these protective measures are widely applied.

The viewpoints in *Current Controversies: Cyberterrorism* offer expert opinions on the many angles of this troubling issue. They explore the role governments, cybersecurity firms, and individuals play in preventing cyberterrorism and what steps can be taken once an attack has occurred from a range of perspectives. Although there is much that is unknown—and potentially unknowable—when it comes to cyberterrorism, these viewpoints offer greater clarity on this complex problem facing contemporary society.

Notes

1. History.com editors, "Patriot Act," History.com, August 21, 2018, https://www .history.com/topics/21st-century/patriot-act.

2. "Creation of the Department of Homeland Security," Department of Homeland Security, September 24, 2015, https://www.dhs.gov/creation-department -homeland-security.

3. Ian Traynor, "Russia Accused of Unleashing Cyberwar to Disable Estonia," *Guardian*, May 16, 2007, https://www.theguardian.com/world/2007/may/17 /topstories3.russia.

4. Megan Brenan, "Cyberterrorism Tops List of 11 Potential Threats to US," Gallup, March 22, 2021, https://news.gallup.com/poll/339974/cyberterrorism -tops-list-potential-threats.aspx.

5. Lee Jarvis and Stuart Macdonald, "What Is Cyberterrorism and Why Does It Matter? Findings from a Survey of Researchers," *Terrorism and Political Violence,* May 8, 2014, https://www.tandfonline.com/doi/abs/10.1080/0954655 3.2013.847827#.U7Mw0_ldWV0.

6. Anna-Maria Talihärm, "Cyberterrorism: In Theory or in Practice?" *Defense Against Terrorism Review*, Fall 2010, qtd. in Lee Jarvis and Stuart Macdonald, "What Is Cyberterrorism and Why Does It Matter? Findings from a Survey of Researchers," *Terrorism and Political Violence,* May 8, 2014, https://www .tandfonline.com/doi/abs/10.1080/09546553.2013.847827#.U7Mw0_ldWV0.

7. Gabriel Weimann, "Cyberterrorism: How Real Is the Threat?" United States Institute of Peace, December 2004, https://www.usip.org/sites/default/files /sr119.pdf.

8. Stefan Soesanto, "Cyber Terrorism. Why it exists, why it doesn't, and why it will," Real Instituto Elcano, April 17, 2020, http://www.realinstitutoelcano.org /wps/portal/rielcano_en/contenido?WCM_GLOBAL_CONTEXT=/elcano /elcano_in/zonas_in/ari47-2020-soesanto-cyber-terrorism-why-it-exists-why -it-doesnt-and-why-it-will.

9. Dale L. Watson, "The Terrorist Threat Confronting the United States," FBI, February 6, 2002, https://archives.fbi.gov/archives/news/testimony/the -terrorist-threat-confronting-the-united-states.

10. Ronen Bergman and Mark Mazzetti, "The Secret History of the Push to Strike Iran," *New York Times Magazine*, September 4, 2019, https://www.nytimes .com/2019/09/04/magazine/iran-strike-israel-america.html.

11. Sue Marquette Poremba, "Cyber Terrorist Threats Loom 10 Years After 9/11," NBC News, September 6, 2011, https://www.nbcnews.com/id/wbna44415109.

12. Ellen Nakashima, "US Accuses Hacker of Stealing Military Members' Data and Giving It to ISIS," *Washington Post*, October 16, 2015, https://www .washingtonpost.com/world/national-security/in-a-first-us-charges-a -suspect-with-terrorism-and-hacking/2015/10/15/463447a8-738b-11e5-8248 -98e0f5a2e830_story.html.

CHAPTER 1

Is Cyberterrorism Distinct from Cyberwarfare and Other Cyberattacks?

Overview: There Are Many Variables to Consider When Defining Cyberterrorism

Fawzia Cassim

Fawzia Cassim is associate professor in the Department of Criminal and Procedural Law at the University of South Africa.

Cyber space is regarded as the meeting place for criminal groups.[1] Cyber space has recently emerged as the latest battleground in this digital age.[2] The convergence of the physical and virtual worlds has resulted in the creation of a "new threat" called cyber terrorism.[3] Before 9/11, much apprehension arose about the threat of cyber terrorism including fears about a "digital Pearl Harbour."[4] The millennium bug further enhanced this fear.[5] In the context of post 9/11, the threat of cyber terrorism is often linked to Al-Qaeda and other terrorist organisations.[6] Cyber terrorists are regarded as computer savvy individuals who look for vulnerabilities that can be easily exploited.[7] Cyber terrorism is one of the recognised cyber crimes.[8] It has been defined as the "premeditated use of disruptive activities, or the threat thereof, in cyber space, with the intention to further social, ideological, religious, political or similar objectives, or to intimidate any person in the furtherance of such objectives.[9] Usually such attacks can take different forms: a terrorist could break into a company's computer network causing havoc, sabotage a country's gas lines or wreak havoc on the international finance system.[10] These terrorist attacks against information infrastructures, computer systems, computer programmes and data may cause injury, loss of life and destruction of property. The aim of such unlawful attacks is to intimidate or persuade a government or its people to further a political or social objective.[11] Cyber attack methods are also said to possess many

"Addressing the Spectre of Cyber Terrorism: A Comparative Perspective," by F. Cassim, Potchefstroom Electronic Law Journal (PELJ), 15(2), 1-37. http://www.scielo.org.za/scielo .php?script=sci_arttext&pid=S1727-37812012000200015&lng=en&tlng=en. Licensed under CC BY-SA 4.0.

advantages over conventional methods of terrorism.[12] However, distinctions should be drawn between hacktivism and cyber terrorism, and the use of digital means for organisational purposes and the use of digital communications to actually commit acts of terror.[13]

The horrific events of 9/11 provided the impetus for many countries to introduce anti-terrorist legislation. Such anti-terrorist legislation not only focuses on legislation to criminalise cyber terrorist activity and impose penalties proportional to the act but also to prevent cyber terrorist activity or mitigate its impact by denying cyber terrorists materials, finance, support and equipment. The September 11 attacks illustrated that terrorism crosses national and ethnic boundaries and changed the prevailing attitudes to terrorism.[14]

[…]

Definition of Cyber Terrorism

Terrorists are said to use the Internet to spread propaganda and conduct internal communications. However, threats resulting from terrorist use of the Internet have been strongly debated. According to Phillip Brunst, the difference in opinion is due to a lack of exact terminology about the term "cyber terrorism."[17] Maura Conway defines cyber terrorism as "acts of terrorism carried out using the Internet and /or against Internet infrastructures."[18] Dorothy Denning defines cyber terrorism as "the convergence of terrorism and cyberspace. It is understood to mean unlawful attacks and threats of attack against computers, networks and the information stored therein when done to intimidate or coerce a government or its people in the furtherance of political or social objectives."[19] Mark Pollit defines cyber terrorism as a "premeditated, politically motivated attack against information, computer systems, computer programmes, and data which result in violence against noncombatant targets by sub national groups or clandestine agents."[20] Such attacks may lead to death or bodily injury, or cause explosions, plane crashes, water contamination, severe economic loss or serious attacks against critical infrastructure.[21] Cyber terrorism encompasses attacks against life and electronic infrastructure which are directed against national security establishments and critical infrastructure.[22] The aim of the attacks is to cause a state of terror and panic in the general public. Terrorists may also use information technology to perpetrate new offences or exploit cyber space to commit more traditional activities such as planning, intelligence, logistical capabilities and finance.[23] Thus, terrorists may use computer technology to secure many of their organisational goals. However, attacks that disrupt nonessential services or present a costly nuisance do not amount to cyber terrorism.[24] Denning also maintains that while terrorists may use cyber space to facilitate traditional forms of terrorism such as bombings, or use the Internet to spread their messages and recruit supporters, there are few indications that they are actually pursuing cyber terrorism.[25] However, this could change in the future.

The blurring of the distinction between hacktivism and cyber terrorism has also fuelled the debate on cyber terrorism. The term "hacking" refers to the use of special software and techniques of a disruptive nature ("hacking tools") to exploit computers.[26] However, Peter Krapp maintains that hacktivists should not be regarded as secret agents, soldiers, terrorists or net warriors but rather as individuals or groups who strive to capture attention and achieve maximum media effect in their quest to raise the awareness of citizens regarding certain rights and liberties.[27] It is debatable whether hacktivists will succeed in changing government policy.[28] Nevertheless, hacktivism should be distinguished from cyber terrorism.

Different Uses of the Internet by Terrorist Groups

Organised crime and terrorist groups are using sophisticated computer technology to bypass government detection and carry out destructive acts of violence. The actions of Rami Yousef, who orchestrated the 1993 World Trade Center bombing by using encryption to store details of his scheme on his laptop computer, is a case in point.[29] It has also been reported that the first known attack by terrorists against a country's computer system took place in Sri Lanka in 1998, when the ethnic Tamil Tiger guerrillas overwhelmed Sri Lankan embassies with 800 e-mails a day over a two-week period.[30] These messages threatened massive disruption of communications, and caused fear and panic among ordinary Sri Lankans as the rebel group was notorious for killing people. During the war in Kosovo in 1999, Serb sympathisers tried to target the NATO website with viruses.[31] In another incident, cyber attacks were launched against the Estonian state during April 2007. The targets were the Estonian Parliament, banks, media houses and government departments. These attacks affected critical services.[32] The events in Estonia illustrated how countries can be put at risk by attacks via the Internet.[33] Thus computers have been used as tools by terrorists to execute terror attacks and advance their particular agendas.[34] However, there is "little concrete evidence" to demonstrate that cyber terrorism has resulted in a catastrophic loss of life or physical destruction often associated with conventional terrorism.[35]

On the other hand, terrorists can also use the Internet for organisational purposes rather than to commit acts of terror. Terrorists can use the computer to commit various crimes such as identity theft, computer viruses, hacking, malware, destruction or manipulation of data.[36] Terrorists can use information communication technologies (ICTs) and the Internet for different purposes: propaganda, information gathering, preparation of real-world attacks, publication of training material, communication, terrorist financing and attacks against critical infrastructures.[37] This means that organisations or governments which depend on the operation of computers and computer networks can be easily attacked. The Internet has the advantage of being "a more immediate, individual, dynamic, in-depth, interactive, anonymous, unedited, cheaper and far-reaching process than conventional media."[38] These factors facilitate the task of terrorists to execute their plans unhindered.[39] Information on how to make bombs is also freely available on the Internet.[40] However, it should be borne in mind that "terrorist use of computers as a facilitator of their activities, whether for propaganda, recruitment, communication or other purposes is simply not cyber terrorism."[41] Similarly, protest action by way of "virtual sit-ins" on websites (called electronic civil disobedience) does not amount to cyber terrorism.[42]

Cyber Terrorism: Myth or Reality?

Although cyber terrorism has become a more dominant force in the global battle between information and network warfare, much misconception still exists over what cyber terrorism entails. As stated earlier, it is important to recognise that all "cyberspace-based threats" are not necessarily terrorism.[43] According to Stohl, the concern with the threat of cyber terrorism stems from a combination of fear and ignorance.[44] Stohl maintains that the discussion about cyber security also involves some misinformation and the exploitation of fears of the general public.[45] The failure to distinguish between hacktivism and cyber terrorism has also contributed to the fear and hype about the threat of cyber terrorism.[46] Some writers believe that the media has also exaggerated the possibility of cyber terrorist attacks causing much concern and panic in the public domain.[47] However, the number of potential targets and the lack of proper and adequate safeguards have also made addressing the threat a daunting task. One should also not underestimate the risk and potential of future threats.[48] Thus, a need arises for the re-examination of commonly held beliefs about the nature of computer systems and cyber terrorism.[49] To this end, measures to address cyber security, to introduce adequate cyber terrorist legislation and to make software safe and effective should be introduced. One should also bear in mind that the removal of technical information from the Internet (such as information on how to execute terror attacks) does not provide an adequate guarantee to safeguard the Internet as such material can be easily loaded onto offshore or other international servers.[50] Gordon and

Ford maintain that an urgent need arises for the development of minimum standards of security for computer networks.[51] They also endorse the idea of negotiations to resolve long-standing disputes with terrorist groups, the careful use of surveillance techniques to gather information on terrorist communications and the sharing of information across various public and private sectors to combat terrorism.[52]

[…]

Since September 11, concerns about cyber terrorism in the United States have multiplied.[53] The USA Patriot Act of 2001 was enacted by President George Bush in response to the 9/11 attacks on the World Trade Centre and Pentagon.[54] Although the USA Patriot Act addresses several issues, certain key provisions relate to cyber security and other computer concerns. To this end, the Act has eased restrictions on electronic surveillance to facilitate the capture of terrorists.[55] The Act also contains anti-money laundering provisions in order to prevent terrorists from achieving any financial gain from their actions.[56] The Patriot Act also includes terrorism and computer crimes on its list of offences.[57] However, the Act has been criticised for violating the civil rights of ordinary American citizens.[58]

Cyber terrorists are said to have the ability to cripple critical infrastructure such as communication, energy and government operations. Cell phones have also been used to track terrorists and to provide evidence against them.[59] Terrorist websites are also under increased surveillance since 9/11 to strengthen the fight against terrorism.[60] A call has also been made for the development of cyber intelligence as a better co-ordinated government discipline to predict computer-related threats and deter them.[61]

[…]

Recommendations and Conclusions

The debate about the threat that cyber terrorism poses will continue into the future. Cyber terrorism is a global menace which requires a united, global response. One should not underestimate the risks and potential of future threats. Countries must work together to introduce a set of core consensus crimes that can be enforceable against cyber criminals in any jurisdiction.[115] The events in Estonia during 2007 demonstrated that governments are vulnerable to attacks by digital means. Every state should enact legislation denying cyber terrorists "safe havens" and safe places of operation. However, "law alone is insufficient; it must be buttressed with faithful enforcement and effective prevention strategies."[116] Therefore, it is also important to build defences against cyber criminals and cyber terrorists. The convergence of terrorism and the cyber world has created a new threat that has to be taken seriously.[117]

[…]

It is submitted that this problem can be addressed not only though enacting stringent legislation and enhancing cyber security measures but also through international cooperation. Although the global fight against cyber terrorism is necessary, combating cyber terrorism should not jeopardise basic human rights and fundamental freedoms. To this end, "the urge to restrict, prohibit and to curtail must be resisted."[118] Therefore, countries need to ensure that a balance is maintained between the protection of human rights and the need for effective prosecution. The following steps should be taken by countries to combat the spectre of cyber terrorism globally:

- Countries should ensure that its cyber terrorism legislation is compatible with international human rights instruments. …
- Countries should educate the public about the threat of cyber terrorism as vigilance is a key factor in addressing the potential threat of cyber terrorism. Users of the Internet should also be encouraged to adopt stronger security measures.
- The role of the media is critical in the fight against cyber terrorism. The media should follow a concise and sensible approach rather than exploit the fears of the ordinary public.
- Countries should regulate cyber cafés as these cafés are popular Internet access points.

- Countries should explore the feasibility of introducing Internet filtering measures to control access to websites that pose serious threats to their national security.
- Countries should introduce specialised law enforcement and training skills, and improve computer forensic capabilities. The respective governments must also initiate support and training within government, with the help of the private sector and international enterprises. Crime and corruption at various government departments should also be rooted out.
- Countries should develop cyber intelligence as a new and better co-ordinated government discipline to predict computer-related threats and deter them.
- Countries should enter into partnerships with other countries to provide technical and material support and increase cooperation among the intelligence agencies of different countries to facilitate exchange of sensitive information to counter cyber terrorist threats. International cooperation is important to ensure the integrity of the Internet. There should also be cooperation to secure networks.
- Countries should encourage reconciliation and respect for diversity, and bridge gulfs between different countries in the broader international community to counteract terrorist threats. To this end, negotiations should be explored as a way to resolve long-standing disputes. A country should also engage all its citizens in its counter terrorist strategies.
- Countries should keep pace with evolving technology to counteract potential cyber terrorist threats. New technologies need to be developed and enhanced in the global fight against terrorism.

Endnotes

1. Tushabe and Baryamureeba 2005 *World Academy of Science, Engineering and Technology* 66.

2. Veerasamy 2009 *4th International Conference on Information Warfare and Security* 26-27 March.

3. It should be noted that the physical world refers to the place where we live and function, whilst the virtual world refers to the place in which computer programmes function.

4. The term "electronic or digital Pearl Harbour" was first coined by tech writer Winn Schwartau in 1991. See further, Stohl 2006 *Crime Law and Social Change* http://ceps.anu.edu.au/publications /pdfs/stohl.

5. The millennium bug, which is also referred to as the Y2K problem, was the result of an outdated programming system which had not accounted for the transition from 1999 to 2000. Of course, this problem soon came to pass without any major catastrophe. *Ibid.*

6. *Ibid.*

7. Raghavan 2003 *Journal of Law, Technology and Policy* 297.

8. It is important to distinguish between cyber crime and cyber terrorism. Cyber terrorism is usually restricted to activities which have a cyber component and the common components of terrorism. Therefore, it is submitted that a discussion of cyber terrorism cannot be divorced from a discussion of terrorism as the two concepts are linked together. This article will focus on cyber terrorism. However, it will also touch on terrorism where relevant.

9. Tushabe & Baryamureeba (n 1) 66-67. Also see Denning 2002 http://www .iwar.org.uk/cyberterror/resources/denning.htm.

10. Guru & Mahishwar "Terror networking" 71.

11. *Ibid.*

12. Terrorists find cyber attack methods to be cheaper than traditional methods; the actions can be difficult to track or trace; the actions can be done remotely anywhere in the world; a number of targets can be attacked effortlessly and it can affect a large number of people. See Garg "Cyber terrorism" 121. Also see Brunst 2010 "Terrorism and the Internet" 53-56.

13. See Stohl 2006 (n 4) 1. Also see Krapp 2005 *Grey Room Inc and Massachusetts Institute of Technology* 70-93.

14. Young 2006 *Boston College International and Comparative Law Review* 23-103 29.

17. Brunst also maintains that the use of additional terminology such as "digital Pearl Harbour," "electronic Waterloo" and "electronic Chernobyl" which focus on possible future attacks by terrorists, has further complicated matters. See Brunst (n 12) 51.

18. Conway 2007 "Terrorism and the New Media" 1.

19. Denning (n 9) 2. Stohl sees no reason to reject Denning's definition. See Stohl (n 4) 8. Also see Gordon & Ford 2002 http://www.symantec.com/avcenter /reference/cyberterrorism.

20. Pollit 1998 http://www.scribd.com/doc/; Also see Goodman & Brenner 2002 *International Journal of Law and Information Technology* 150. However, Phillip Brunst regards Pollit's definition as being a narrow definition of cyber

terrorism. He maintains that a broad definition of cyber terrorism might include other forms of terrorist use of the Internet. See Brunst (n 12) 51.

21. Gordon & Ford (n 19) 4; Goodman & Brenner (n 20) 145; Denning (n 9) 2. Also see Brunst (n 12) 66.

22. Goodman & Brenner (n 20). Weimann maintains that cyber terrorism involves the use of computer network tools to harm or shut down critical national infrastructures such as energy, transportation and government operations. Weimann 2005 *Studies in Conflict and Terrorism* 130.

23. *Ibid.*

24. Denning (n 9) 2.

25. Conventional terrorism is said to have a "greater dramatic effect" than cyber terrorism. Denning (n 9) 19-20; 22. Also see Stohl (n 4) 8; 11-13. However, Brunst reports that although many attacks have taken place, they have been kept confidential to avoid security lapses or breaches if such details were published. See Brunst (n 12) 53.

26. Hacktivism includes electronic civil disobedience. For more information, see Denning (n 9)12.

27. Krapp (n 13) 86-88. Also see Brunst (n 12) 56-57, regarding the blurring of the distinction between the terms "hacktivism" and "cyber terrorism."

28. Denning (n 9) 22.

29. Bazelon et al. 2006 *The American Criminal Law Review* 306.

30. See Tushabe & Baryamureeba (n 1) 67; Also see Denning (n 9) 7. Also see Walker 2006 "Cyber-Terrorism: United Kingdom" 635.

31. Walker (n 30) 635. Chinese computer hackers also launched attacks on US websites to protest against NATO's bombing of a Chinese embassy in Kosovo. See Krapp (n 13) 72.

32. See Veerasamy "Conceptual Framework" 4. Also see Brunst (n 12) 62.

33. Brunst (n 12) 52.

34. It has also been reported that computers and the Internet played a key role in the execution of the September 11 attacks in that computers were used to make travel plans and purchase air tickets. However, it is submitted that these acts can be distinguished from cyber terrorism in that computers are used here to plan acts of terror rather than to commit acts of terror. See Gordon & Ford (n 19) 4; also see Gerke 2009 "Understanding Cybercrime" http://www.itu.int /ITU-D/cyb/ cybersecurity/legislation/html.

35. Stohl (n 4) 2. Computers are said to be the means to achieve terrorist purposes rather than the objects of attack. See Walker (n 30) 636.

36. "Malware" is the distribution of malicious codes to disrupt computer networks. See Raghavan (n 7) 299-300 regarding the different types of attacks that can be brought against computer networks. Also see Gordon and Ford (n 19) 7.

37. Gerke (n 34) 52-57. Also see Brunst (n 12) 70-73; 74-75; Walker (n 30) 635-642 and Conway (n 18) 4-10.

38. Conway (n 18) 3-4.

39. Raghavan (n 7) 297. It should be stated that the general motivations to commit crimes via the Internet are: the lack of a definite physical location, the use of bandwidth and speed of third parties to perpetrate cyber crimes, the anonymity of cyberspace, the lack of physical borders or boundaries and the cost-benefit ratio. For detailed discussion about these issues, see Brunst (n 12) 53-56.

40. This includes material such as *The Terrorist's Handbook*, *How to Make a Bomb: Book Two* and *The Anarchist's Cookbook*. See Walker (n 30) 645. The Internet also contains detailed instructions on how to establish underground organisations and execute terror attacks. See Conway (n 18) 17.

41. Weimann (n 22) 133. Attacks on critical infrastructure are said to fall under the domain of cyber terrorism. Also see Walker (n 30) 634.

42. For more information on electronic civil disobedience, see Dominguez 2008 Third Text 661-670.

43. For example, attacks on data contained within systems and programmes do not translate to "terrorist" acts. However, in some instances, the distinction between cyber crime (such as hacking) and cyber terrorism has also become blurred. See Brunst (n 12) 56-57.

44. This translates to a fear of technology and the fear of terrorism (both unknown factors). This results in the nature of cyber terrorism being misunderstood. Also see Embar-Seddon 2002 *American Behavioural Scientist* 1033-1043.

45. Stohl (n 4) 5. Also see Conway (n 18) 29.

46. Hacking refers to activities conducted online that aim to reveal, manipulate and exploit vunerabilities in computer operating systems and software. Also see Denning (n 9) 12.

47. Veerasamy (n 2) 1. Also see Green 2002 *Washington Monthly* http://www .washingtonmonthly.com/features/2001/0211.green.html 1-8. Also see Frauenheim (n 15) 2.

48. The lack of a large cyber attack by terrorists should not make one complacent. See Brunst (n 12) 75.

49. Gordon and Ford (n 19) 14.

50. Conway (n 18) 19.

51. Gordon and Ford (n 19) 12.

52. *Ibid*.

53. The September 11 hijackings led to an outcry that airliners are susceptible to cyber terrorism. See Green (n 47) 4.

54. The USA Patriot Act stands for: Uniting and Strengthening America by Providing Appropriate Tools Required to Intercept and Obstruct Terrorism.

See Young (n 14) 75-76. Also Raghavan (n 7) 298; 304. The law protects the national infrastructure by easing the restrictions placed on electronic surveillance by amending provisions of the Computer Fraud and Abuse Act 1986 to increase penalties for cybercrimes.

55. The Act has expanded the powers of the federal government to combat terrorism in the area of surveillance and interception of communications; it provides for closer policing of financial transactions; it strengthens the anti-money laundering regulations to disrupt terrorist funding opportunities and it authorizes administrative detentions. See Young (n 14) 76. Alse see Raghavan (n 7) 305.

56. See ss 301-77. Raghavan (n 7) 305.

57. See s 814. The increase in vigilance against the threat of cyber terrorism has resulted in increased penalties for all forms of computer hacking including hacktivist activity. See Dominguez (n 42) 664.

58. To illustrate this, the expanded surveillance measure in the Act has been criticised because of its lack of adequate checks and balances. The government's ability to spy on suspected computer trespassers without a court order has also been criticised as it infringes on the civil liberties of suspected trespassers. Raghavan (n 7) 310.

59. Walker (n 30) 664. It is noteworthy that South Africa has introduced the Regulation of Interception of Communication Act 2002 (RICA) for this purpose. For further information on RICA, see the discussion in section 6.4 below.

60. Conway (n 18) 22-23; 28.

61. Anonymous 2011 http://www.eLaw@legalbrief.co.za.

115. See Goodman & Brenner (n 20) 223.

116. See Young (n 14) 28.

117. See Brunst (n 12) 76.

118. See Walker (n 30) 663. As stated earlier, measures taken in the United States, the United Kingdom and India have all been criticised by human rights campaigners.

Cyberterrorism Encompasses a Range of Online Activities That Support Terrorism

Laura Mayer Lux

Laura Mayer Lux is a lawyer and academic researcher with the faculty of law at the Pontificia Universidad Católica de Valparaíso in Chile. Her research includes work on fraud and computer crimes, among other criminal activity.

The term "cyberterrorism" is complex and combines two concepts: "cyber," referring to cyberspace, and "terrorism," whose meaning and scope will be analyzed later. On this basis, we can assume that cyberterrorism is a special type of terrorism, where the "place" or "medium" it is carried out in is cyberspace (Conway, 2014; Denning, 2000). Cyberspace is considered "a globally interconnected network of digital information and communications infrastructures" (Melzer, 2011: 4), normally understood to mean the internet and, more broadly, computer networks (Ambos, 2015; Yannakogeorgos, 2014).

The concept of cyberterrorism usually refers to a range of very different actions, from the simple spread of propaganda online, to the alteration or destruction of information, and even to the planning and carrying out of terrorist attacks via the use of computer networks. As such, in order to better understand what cyberterrorism is, this article will begin by analyzing the concept of "terrorism"—including its structure, harm principle, and elements— as a broad category to which the species "cyberterrorism" belongs; later, it will delimit the idea of cyberterrorism and distinguish it from others with which it has a certain similarity; finally, it will raise some of the most important challenges that cyberterrorism implies in a global and technologically interconnected world.

[…]

What Is Cyberterrorism?

Much has also been written on the topic of cyberterrorism, despite lacking a unanimous consensus regarding its scope and meaning. As it were, for cyberterrorism to be, effectively, a form of terrorism, it must meet the structure, harm principle and elements of terrorism. As a result, the scope of cyberterrorism is, as its name suggests, based on the "place" in which it occurs or the "medium" through which it is carried out: in cyberspace instead of the physical world. From this point of view, cyberterrorism is not an autonomous crime, which should be punished independently. Rather, it implies a kind of terrorism characterized by a unique method of execution.

That cyberterrorism is defined by its location or the medium through which it is executed can be criticized to some extent. To address such criticisms, a comparison can be made to aircraft hijacking terrorist acts, such as the 9/11 terrorist attacks on the World Trade Center; or vehicle-based terrorist attacks, such as when a truck deliberately drove into a crowd of people on the Nice promenade in 2016. In reality, the scope of cyberterrorism appears to follow the general tendency for many "real world" phenomena to be replicated online. Thus, it is common to talk about "cyber activism" (Milan and Hintz, 2013) as a type of activism carried out online; or "cyberbullying" (Kraft and Wang, 2009) being a type of bullying which also occurs online. Similarly, it's not difficult to imagine that, with the rise of terrorism, there has also emerged its virtual strain: cyberterrorism.

The (Cyber)terrorists' Actions and the (Cyber)terrorists' Author

The Continental European tradition of criminal law usually differentiates between what an individual does (in other words, their behavior) and who they are (in other words, their character, personal preferences, thoughts, etc.) From this, we can distinguish between the criminal law of "acts" or "facts" (Mir Puig, 2016), consistent with a liberal criminal justice system, and the criminal law of "author" (Velásquez Velásquez, 2009), consistent with an authoritarian criminal justice system. The criminal law of "acts" is based on actions, such as theft or sexual abuse of a minor. The criminal law of "author" is based on dangerous criminal personality traits, such as if an individual is a thief or pedophile. At its core, under the criminal law of "author," a thief or pedophile is marked by a kind of stigma, wherein independent of their actions, and even though their theft or sexual abuse of minors is now in the past, they will forever be considered a thief or pedophile. This is linked to the concept of criminal law of "the enemy" (Jakobs, 2003), which treats those breaching the rules as enemies of the state rather than citizens "who are simply a source of danger that must be eliminated by any means, whatever the cost" (Cancio Meliá, 2002: 20).

That same form of discussion and analysis is often seen when discussing terrorism, where a (political) opponent is, strategically, labelled a "terrorist" (Mañalich, 2017). In such an approach, commonly seen as authoritarian or anti-liberal, the focus is on the "terrorist." Meanwhile, a liberal approach focuses on the actions of the so-called terrorist more than their personal characteristics as a "terrorist."

The final approach to responding to terrorism is the correct one because, amongst other things, not all actions of a "terrorist" or by a member of a terrorist organization can be classified as terrorism or terrorist acts. In reality, a "terrorist" is far more likely to engage in a wide variety of activities ranging from non-criminal (such as spending time with family or driving a car), to committing non-terrorist crimes (such as fraud or drug trafficking), than to actual terrorist attacks (such as bombing the seat of government.)

The same applies to cyberterrorism. That is, an authoritarian or anti-liberal criminal law would focus on the "cyberterrorist," whereas a liberal criminal law would focus on the actions of the so-called cyberterrorist more than their personal characteristics as a "cyberterrorist." Just like a "terrorist," a "cyberterrorist" can also engage in a wide range of activities online, ranging from non-criminal, to criminal but not terrorist, through to terrorist in nature.

However, it is possible to distinguish between two kinds of "cyberterrorist": The first kind, likely to be more common, is the traditional "terrorist" that uses the internet as well as information and communication technologies to perpetrate their attacks. In this case, those carrying out traditional terrorist attacks take advantage of the benefits offered by these technological tools, for example the ability to negatively impact a large number of people in a brief period of time without personally physically exposing oneself (Weimann, 2005), but from the comfort of their own computer. This applies both in the preparation of crime (planning, conspiracy, etc.) and to their partial execution (attempted crime) or completion (successful crime). In the case of attacks that make some use of technology, a terrorist can, amongst other things, attack the networks that allow for control and supervision of industrial processes, systems known as SCADA (Supervisory Control And Data Acquisition) (Poveda Criado and Torrente Barredo, 2016); or, damage "critical infrastructure" (Gercke and Brunst, 2009; Von Bubnoff, 2003), for example the water supply and potable water, means of transport and telecommunications, health services, etc., which in turn affect a considerable number of people.

The second kind is the subject falling within the "hacker" archetype who begins executing actions of escalating intensity: first by destroying data of actual users; then sabotaging information stored by a (large) company or (large) government entity; finally directing an attack against a SCADA or critical infrastructure through the use of technology. In this final case, we exit the scope of mere hacking and enter into cyberterrorism, as long as all the requirements (structure, harm principle, elements) are present which comprise actual terrorism. Assuming that there is a debate along the lines of what exactly is implied by hacking (Madarie, 2017), its definition can be derived from cyberterrorism's through exclusion. That is to say, it would be cyberterrorism if actions are executed "on" or "through the medium of" cyberspace and the required structure, harm principle and elements that characterize terrorism are present. If those requirements do not exist in practice, it may be a case of hacking or hacktivism (Hampson, 2012). For this reason, it can be said that cyberterrorism is always one step beyond mere hacking or hacktivism (Gillespie, 2016).

Notwithstanding this, it is possible to imagine links between hackers and organized crime, particularly terrorism. Beyond the situations where terrorists count hackers within its ranks—in which case it can be difficult to differentiate between (cyber)terrorism and hacking—it remains possible for hackers to be motivated by profit and to contact terrorist groups in order to sell their computer skills or software that could be used in terrorist attacks (Wilson, 2003). Or, that members of a terrorist group turn to hackers whenever they seek to use cyberspace or technologies to commit an attack that they are not in a position to carry out themselves because they lack the necessary skills. As has been outlined in relation to terrorism (Mañalich, 2017), in these cases it should be possible to distinguish between the role played by the members of the terrorist organizations—"from within"—and that played by their supporters (in this case hackers)—"from outside"—whose relevance in the criminal justice system depends on the impact they have on the existence and operations of the organization.

(Cyber)criminality and (Cyber)terrorism

In the same way that any crime should not be confused with a terrorist attack (Poveda Criado and Torrente Barredo, 2016), the concept of cybercrime should not be confused with that of cyberterrorism (Weimann, 2005). In that sense and as already indicated, just as terrorism is always more severe than other forms of criminality, cyberterrorism is always more severe than other behaviors that are carried out "in" or "through" cyberspace. This approach seeks to avoid a "trivialization" of the concept of terrorism (Mañalich, 2015) and cyberterrorism, which would certainly occur if they were defined without considering the particular severity that characterizes both phenomena.

In order to better understand what has been pointed out, we must take into account not only the concepts of terrorism and cyberterrorism, in the aforementioned sense, but also the notions of computer crime, cybercrime, and common crime. It should be noted that although not all authors distinguish between computer crime and cybercrime, differentiating between them can be useful for analytical purposes.

Computer crimes can be classified into computer crimes in a broad sense and computer crimes in a strict sense. Computer crimes in a broad sense (Lara, Martínez and Viollier, 2014) are traditional crimes that are committed through computer mechanisms or the internet. Respectively, information and communication technologies have expanded the contexts or means of execution of certain traditional crimes, such as fraud (Gercke and Brunst, 2009) or sexual abuse (Clough, 2010), which can now also be committed through computers or the internet. Consequently, computer crime in a broad sense has also been called crime committed "through" computer systems (Marberth-Kubicki, 2010).

Computer crimes in a strict sense (D'Aiuto and Levita, 2012), on the other hand, are new crimes committed towards computer systems or the internet. Generally, these are actions that are directed against software. For this reason, this phenomenon has also been labeled as crime committed "against" computer systems (Marberth-Kubicki, 2010). This usually includes crimes such as computer sabotage (destruction or disablement of data or software), computer espionage (unlawful access or obtaining of data or software) and computer fraud (alteration or manipulation of data or software) (Jijena, 2008).

Cybercrimes are computer crimes (in a broad or strict sense) that are committed through the internet (Cárdenas Aravena, 2008; Clough, 2010). Unlike computer crimes, which are perpetrated "through" or "against" computer systems, cybercrimes are always carried out in a specific context: cyberspace. In this sense, what defines a cybercrime is not its commission through or against a computer system, but a specific "place" or "medium" of perpetration.

The categories "computer crime" and "cybercrime" are not mutually exclusive and can be present together. Therefore, the diffusion of child pornography through the internet constitutes a cybercrime and a computer crime in a broad sense, whereas the destruction of data from computer systems carried out in cyberspace constitutes a cybercrime and a computer crime in a strict sense.

Finally, common crimes are all those that cannot be classified as computer crimes or cybercrimes, or in any other way in particular. Thus, their definition is always determined by process of elimination. For example, theft is a common crime, in the same way that homicide is. If those crimes are committed by means of a drone operated by radio control, they do not classify as cybercrimes. The radio control is a closed system and so it lies outside of the internet. Although both examples can be committed using technology, they escape the phenomenon of computing or execution in cyberspace.

A subject that belongs to a terrorist organization can carry out all the activities discussed above, that is, computer crimes (in a broad or strict sense), cybercrimes or common crimes. In order to be classified as terrorist behavior however, the structure, harm principle and elements of terrorism need to be present. For cyberterrorism, moreover, terrorist behavior must be carried out "in" or "through" cyberspace.

Consequently, not all computer crimes (in a broad or strict sense) committed by a "terrorist" constitute terrorism or cyberterrorism. Not all the cybercrimes executed by someone belonging to a terrorist organization is to be described as terrorism or cyberterrorism. And, certainly, not all common crimes carried out by a "terrorist" are meant to be thought of as terrorism or cyberterrorism.

Neither is cyberterrorism configured when someone who belongs to a terrorist organization commits a terrorist act using technologies other than computer networks. For example, an organization that puts a bomb in a hospital full of patients where the trigger is a mobile phone activated through a telephone call. If that organization carries out such an attack in order to destabilize the democratic constitutional order, its behavior may be described as terrorism, but not cyberterrorism, since it was not executed in cyberspace or using computer networks.

The Real Cyberterrorism

So far, some problems have been described by the use of the term "cyberterrorism," as well as certain criminal behaviors that do not constitute cyberterrorism. Subsequently, some of the assumptions that correspond to cyberterrorism actions will be described, in order to specify the definition of this concept.

As previously insisted, for cyberterrorism to exist, terrorist behavior must be perpetrated in cyberspace. And for terrorist activities to be executed in cyberspace, it is necessary that the behavior carried out "in" or "through" cyberspace has a structure, a harm principle and the elements that allow it to be classified as such. And all those requirements (structure, harm principle and elements) must be jointly present, otherwise, the conduct in question cannot be considered as cyberterrorism.

In terms of its structure, cyberterrorism is always organized crime, as opposed to individual (cyber)crimes (for example, a computer espionage committed by a single person) or (cyber)crimes carried out by a group on an ad hoc basis (for example, a computer sabotage committed by three individuals: one that develops malware, another that accesses a database and a third that uses malware to destroy certain data).

In effect, although some authors believe in terrorism carried out by a single person and, thus, could also accept individual cyberterrorism, the specific "danger" implied by cyberterrorism, which in part justifies its high punishment in relation to other (cyber)crimes, lies in the existence of an organized collective that operates systematically to commit an indefinite number of crimes. Such danger does not exist in the case of an individual or ad hoc group acting alone, even if they employ similar methods (for example, destruction of critical infrastructure through computer networks) commonly used by cyberterrorist organizations. For the same reason, if a single person gains access to a computer network and modifies the information that is issued and received at the monitoring station of an airport, thereby putting the life or health of people flying on the monitored aircraft at risk, there would certainly be some criminal conduct, but not a cyberterrorist act based on the arguments outlined earlier.

In this context, to speak of a "criminal cyberterrorist association," there would have to exist, as with terrorism, a set number of members, access to resources and funding, and a capacity to sustainably plan and carry out operations over time.

Unlike in the case of traditional terrorism, the perpetration of terrorist and cyberterrorist attacks through the use of technologies could relativize the requirement that there be an organized collective composed of a certain number of "people." In fact, it is currently possible for a single person to comprise a botnet, that is, a series of computers called bots or zombies previously captured by that person. This capture is done through botware (Kochheim, 2015), malware designed to build botnets, which allows access and remote control of the various computer systems that make up the botnet (Choo, 2007). Due to this, it would be possible for a single controller of several bots or zombies to systematically commit an indefinite number of crimes.

However, that single person will never have the "organizational density" that is characteristic of terrorism, which implies the existence of a structure (of people) for collective decision making, to coordinate and persist over time. In this sense, although the possibility of action by that single person to harm other people is amplified due to a botnet, they are not comparable with those of a real (cyber)terrorist organization, the only structure really capable of keeping those interests protected by (cyber)terrorism in check. The amplification of damages through the use of technologies can be observed in many cybercrimes, but that in itself does not justify classifying the behavior individual subjects as terrorist attacks.

Harm Principle

Regarding the harm principle, cyberterrorism does not directly attack individual interests, that is, those that belong to or serve a specific person or a set group of people. On the contrary, cyberterrorism directly affects a collective interest, an interest that is owned by or serves the general public. As in terrorism, the collective interest directly attacked by cyberterrorism is the democratic constitutional order. Hence, it can be affirmed that cyberterrorism constitutes an attack against institutional, state, or national interests.

Said characteristics distinguish cyberterrorism from common crimes like homicide or assault, but also distinguish cyberterrorism from cybercrimes such as computer fraud, all of which directly affect individual rather than collective interests. In other words, even if cyberterrorism harms or threatens individual interests like the life or health of others, this indirect impact is not its ultimate goal, instead the goal is a direct attack on the democratic constitutional order.

Considering the harm principle described, a wide range of situations can be established, ranging from minor to severe.

First, that only the collective interest of "democratic constitutional order" is threatened. This can happen if an individual joins or forms part of a cyberterrorist organization with a criminal agenda. In this case, for these interests to be at risk, indications that threatening actions against the democratic constitutional order have been taken are necessary.

Second, that the collective interest of "democratic constitutional order" is violated and additionally one or more individual interests are threatened. Such a situation may occur when propaganda is used in cyberspace to destabilize a political regime, in which, for example, the life or health of others is put at risk. As was said with respect to terrorism, the threat in question should be plausible or credible, as cyberterrorist groups utilizing propaganda in cyberspace to make laughable or absurd threats towards others should not be considered cyberterrorism.

Third, that the collective interest of "democratic constitutional order" is violated as much as one or more individual interests. This can happen if a cyberterrorist group, in order to execute a set political agenda, remotely takes control, through a computer network, of a traffic light located on a railway line, and causes two trains in the opposite direction to share the same route, producing, for example, death or injury to its passengers.

[…]

Conclusions

Cyberterrorism is distinguished from terrorism by the "place" in which it is perpetrated or by the "medium" through which it is perpetrated, that is, cyberspace. From this point of view, cyberterrorism is not an autonomous crime, but implies a kind of terrorism characterized by a unique method of execution.

Cyberterrorism must comply with the structure, harm principle and elements that define terrorism. Consequently, if these are not verified, we may be in the presence of a cybercrime and not cyberterrorism (for example a computer sabotage). In terms of its structure, cyberterrorism requires the existence of an organization destined to perpetrate (cyber)terrorist attacks. Regarding its harm principle, cyberterrorism must directly violate a collective interest identified with the democratic constitutional order. In terms of its elements, cyberterrorism must be executed with the specific purpose of altering constitutional order or to topple the legitimately elected government; and must be carried out in a manner appropriate to instill terror in people's minds, establishing a belief that anyone anywhere could be a victim of an attack.

Finally, cyberterrorism creates several challenges in a global and technologically interconnected world. Committing cyberterrorism involves the use of the internet, which offers a series of advantages for those participating in the act. In addition, because the real dimensions and potential of cyberterrorism are not yet clear, reacting with preparation becomes difficult.

Digital Terrorism Really Exists

Donald L. Buresh, PhD, JD

Donald L. Buresh is an expert in cybersecurity and policy.

After 9/11, the two fears of a violent attack and technology were merged into one idea—cyberterrorism. When the political dimension was added to the mix, the debate about national security reached a fever pitch, where al Qaeda was seen to be able to use technology to perpetrate nightmarish kinetic damage. The lack of reliable information, or more importantly, the plethora of misinformation, led to the hysteria that al Qaeda and Iraq were capable of employing cyber tools to disable American defenses. The result was an aggressive American policy to combat cyberwarfare and cyberterrorism, where the FBI requested and obtained from Congress $4.5 billion for infrastructure security and the ability to hire over 1,000 cyber investigators.

Through cyberterrorism against governments, private servers, networks, or other electronic devices, hackers can damage systems using viruses, worms, or Trojans, launching denial-of-service ("DoS") attacks, defacing websites, or even demanding that governments or companies pay substantial ransoms. Examples of cyberterrorism include:

- Global terror networks that disrupt major sites by initiating public nuisances or stopping Internet traffic;
- International cyberterrorists accessing and then disabling or modifying signals to military technology;
- Cyberterrorists targeting critical infrastructure systems such as a water treatment plant or an electrical grid; or
- Cyberespionage carried out by governments or private organizations to spy on intelligence communications.

"Does Digital Terrorism Really Exist?" by Donald L. Buresh, PhD, JD, *Journal of Advanced Forensic Sciences*, 2020. https://openaccesspub.org/jafs/article/1367. Licensed under CC BY-4.0.

Cyberterrorists can employ a variety of methods to attack a network. They may access a network or a server and then wait for an opportune time to strike. A cyberterrorist could steal data rather than damage a network if the information is valuable. For example, in 2015, it was reported that the Chinese stole security clearance information on 22.1 million Americans with security clearances, including employees, contractors, as well as family and friends. Viruses, worms, and other computer malware can jeopardize water supplies, transportation systems, power grids, critical infrastructure, and military systems. For example, in Ukraine, a virus was discovered that disabled the country's power grid. DoS attacks can be conducted against both governments and private companies. For example, one of the more significant DoS attack as of this writing occurred in February 2018, where GitHub, a public source code management service that is used by millions of software developers, experienced an incoming attack traffic rate of 1.3 terabytes per second. Other forms of cyber-attacks include ransomware where computers are held hostage until a specified ransom is paid or phishing attacks where cybercriminals attempt to collect information through email and other means to commit identity theft. Yet another type of cyber-attack can occur, particularly when the state actors are engaging in asymmetric warfare in furtherance of their own ends.

The defenses against cyberterrorism vary depending on the type of attack. The installation of effective anti-virus software, as well as periodically checking systems for the presence of malware, can effectively mitigate cyber-attacks. Even so, constant vigilance is necessary as cybercriminals and cyberterrorists are continually developing new methods to thwart cybersecurity.

In the past decade, there have been three significant cyberterrorism acts that have been extensively covered in the literature. They include the Estonian cyber-attack, the Georgian cyber-attack, and the Ukrainian cyber-attack. These […] cyber-attacks affected large portions of the infrastructures of the countries under consideration. The examples reflect the magnitude of the harm that has occurred in the past, and can occur in the present and future.

[…]

What will the next cyber-attack look like? Will it resemble the Estonian cyber-attack, the Georgian cyber-attack, or the Ukrainian cyber-attack? Will it be like when the Chinese stole security clearance information on 22.1 million Americans with security clearances? Will it be similar to the alleged Russian attack on the Democratic National Convention ("DNC") servers? Will it be comparable to the recent GitHub cyber-attack, where the site experienced an incoming attack traffic rate of 1.3 terabytes per second? Or, will the next major attack be so new and unique that organizational defenses will be helpless to prevent it, mitigate it, or minimize the damages? This is what concerns the public today.

[…]Any new attack will probably be analogous to one or more of the cyber-attacks discussed above. For example, if a cyber-attack were to occur tomorrow, there would be little or no change in the technology. The attack would probably very closely resemble past attacks. The cyber-attack would probably use existing available technology. The technology would likely be computer towers, computer notebooks, and cell phones. There would be almost no change in the availability of the Internet of Things ("IoT") (e.g., computers in automobiles, televisions, refrigerators, microwave ovens, etc.). Thus, a cyber-attack would probably be akin to previous attacks, depending on the existing hardware and software employed by the attackers and available at the target site.

However, in five, 10, or 20 years, the situation may dramatically change. The technology in this future period will probably be entirely different from the technology around us today. First, there is the IoT. Smart devices are being marketed and sold to consumers at a rapid pace. (Johnson, 2018). The IoT will pervasively dominate our economy in the next five to 10 years. These devices will probably possess less than adequate security features because security concerns will likely be brushed aside in a rush to market. Cyber attackers will probably note this situation and then exploit it.

Stuxnet and its variations will play a dramatic role in future cyber-attacks. When Stuxnet was used by the United States government a decade ago to disrupt Iranian centrifuges, a physical machine was involved that stopped working correctly. The child or grandchild of Stuxnet could be employed to modify the actions of physical devices such as automobiles, televisions, refrigerators, or microwave ovens. These devices could be programmed by malware to stop functioning or even to explode. A car is by far the most potentially dangerous of the machines mentioned because it is large, heavy, moves quickly, and may contain a fairly large amount of gasoline, which is volatile. With sophisticated computers inside controlling the operation of an automobile, cars could be employed to run people over, or even explode in crowded areas. A Stuxnet-like virus that infected a car could be programmed to affect specific vehicles that would injure or kill particular individuals. When this type of cyber-attack occurs, under certain conditions, a kinetic response by a government may be entirely appropriate.

When looking 20 years into the future, human beings will probably be physically connected to the Internet via nanotechnology that is implanted into their bodies. This technology could interact with human DNA, causing innumerable issues. For example, a cyber-attack could consist of programming humans to perform actions that they normally would not do by circumventing human free will. If the attack was sufficiently malicious, it might be possible to program humans to attack others or to do nothing when a defensive response would be appropriate. In this case, society could easily resemble a *1984* society or a *Brave New World* society, particularly with the advent of social media and the dark web.

Thus, a future cyber-attack depends on the date and time that the attack occurs as well as the technology involved. Without this information, it is probably impossible to predict with any precision or accuracy what a future cyber-attack will resemble.

[…]

Cyberattacks Are Taken into Consideration on the US Government's State Terror List

Rory Carroll

Rory Carroll is a journalist with the Guardian. He currently serves as the Guardian's Ireland correspondent.

The United States may classify North Korea a state sponsor of terrorism after its "cybervandalism" of Sony Pictures, President Barack Obama has said.

The president said the hack on the Hollywood studio was not an act of war but was "very costly," and could land Pyongyang back on the administration's terror list, a designation lifted by the Bush administration in 2008 during nuclear talks.

"We're going to review those [issues] through a process that's already in place," he told CNN in an interview broadcast on Sunday. "I'll wait to review what the findings are."

Obama spoke as Sony Pictures raised the prospect of releasing *The Interview*, the film which allegedly provoked North Korea's attack, online, possibly via YouTube.

Michael Lynton, the studio's chief executive, said it had "not caved" to the hackers and was considering various options to release the comedy, which stars James Franco and Seth Rogen as journalists who are charged with assassinating North Korea's leader, Kim Jong-un. "We would still like the public to see this movie, absolutely," he told CNN.

North Korea has denied any involvement in last month's hack which crippled Sony's Hollywood studio, and threatened to hit back at the White House and other US targets if Washington sanctions it.

The country's top military body, the National Defence Commission, said in a statement on the country's official news

"US May Put North Korea Back on State Terror List After Sony 'Cybervandalism,'" by Rory Carroll, Guardian News and Media Limited, December 21, 2014. Reprinted by permission.

agency that the army and people "are fully ready to stand in confrontation with the US in all war spaces including cyber warfare space to blow up those citadels."

"Our toughest counteraction will be boldly taken against the White House, the Pentagon and the whole US mainland, the cesspool of terrorism, by far surpassing the 'symmetric counteraction' declared by Obama," it said.

John McCain, the Arizona senator, led Republican calls for a robust response from the US, including a restoration of sanctions lifted under the Bush administration.

"The president does not understand that this is the manifestation of a new form of warfare," McCain said, also on CNN. "When you destroy economies and are able to impose censorship on the world … it's more than vandalism, it's a new form of warfare."

In his interview, which was recorded on Friday, Obama said the hack was not act of war. "It was an act of cybervandalism," he said.

Foreign governments and freelance hackers presented cyberthreats to commerce, he said, adding: "If we set a precedent in which a dictator in another country can disrupt through cyber a company's distribution chain or its products, and as a consequence we start censoring ourselves, that's a problem."

The hack was a challenge to the news media as well as the entertainment industry, he said. "CNN has done critical stories about North Korea. What happens if in fact there is a breach in CNN's cyberspace? Are we going to suddenly say, are we not going to report on North Korea?"

Restoring North Korea to the terrorism sponsorship list could be difficult. The State Department would have to determine that the regime repeatedly supported acts of international terrorism, something traditionally understood to mean violent, physical attacks rather than hacking.

Obama and Hollywood's creative community last week accused Sony of surrendering to intimidation and setting a precedent for censorship by cancelling the planned Christmas Day release of *The*

Interview. The studio responded by blaming cinema chains which refused to show the film following anonymous terrorist threats.

The president expressed sympathy for Sony's plight but renewed his claim that he might have been able to help if given the chance: "You know, had they talked to me directly about this decision, I might have called the movie theater chains and distributors and asked them what that story was."

On Saturday, it was reported that the US was seeking China's help in containing North Korea.

Lynton said Sony Pictures still wanted to show the film—a shift in tone from last week when a spokesman said there were no plans for any release—but so far had been stymied by cinema chains and online distributors.

"We have not given in. And we have not backed down. We have always had every desire to have the American public see this movie," he said, adding that the company was exploring all options, including YouTube.

The *Los Angeles Times* on Sunday quoted film industry analysts speculating that Sony Pictures' parent corporation in Japan may sell the studio, a relatively small part of its global operations, in order to get rid of the headache.

There Is Too Much Overlap Between Different Types of Cyberattacks to Effectively Distinguish Them

Catherine A. Theohary and John W. Rollins

Catherine A. Theohary is an information operations and national security specialist at the Congressional Research Service, where John W. Rollins is also a specialist in terrorism and national security. Rollins teaches at numerous universities and routinely advises federal, state, and local governments and private sector corporations on security related matters.

"Cyberattack" is a relatively recent term that can refer to a range of activities conducted through the use of information and communications technology (ICT). The use of distributed denial of service (DDoS) attacks has become a widespread method of achieving political ends through the disruption of online services. In these types of attacks, a server is overwhelmed with Internet traffic so access to a particular website is degraded or denied. The advent of the Stuxnet worm, which some consider the first cyberweapon, showed that cyberattacks may have a more destructive and lasting effect. Appearing to target Iran, Stuxnet malware attacked the computerized industrial control systems on which nuclear centrifuges operate, causing them to self-destruct.

Recent international events have raised questions on when a cyberattack could be considered an act of war, and what sorts of response options are available to victim nations. Although there is no clear doctrinal definition of "cyberwarfare," it is typically conceptualized as state-on-state action equivalent to an armed attack or use of force in cyberspace that may trigger a military response with a proportional kinetic use of force.

"Cyberwarfare and Cyberterrorism: In Brief," by Catherine A. Theohary and John W. Rollins, Federation of American Scientists, March 27, 2015. Reprinted by permission.

Cyberterrorism can be considered "the premeditated use of disruptive activities, or the threat thereof, against computers and/or networks, with the intention to cause harm or further social, ideological, religious, political or similar objectives, or to intimidate any person in furtherance of such objectives." Cybercrime includes unauthorized network breaches and theft of intellectual property and other data; it can be financially motivated, and response is typically the jurisdiction of law enforcement agencies.

The cyberattacks on Sony Entertainment illustrate the difficulties in categorizing attacks and formulating a response policy. On November 24, 2014, Sony experienced a cyberattack that disabled its information technology systems, destroyed data and workstations, and released internal emails and other materials. Warnings surfaced that threatened "9/11-style" terrorist attacks on theaters scheduled to show the film *The Interview*, causing some theaters to cancel screenings and for Sony to cancel its widespread release, although US officials claimed to have "no specific, credible intelligence of such a plot." The Federal Bureau of Investigation (FBI) and the Director of National Intelligence (DNI) attributed the cyberattacks to the North Korean government; North Korea denied involvement in the attack, but praised a hacktivist group, called the "Guardians of Peace," for having done a "righteous deed." During a December 19, 2014, press conference, President Obama pledged to "respond proportionally" to North Korea's alleged cyber assault, "in a place, time and manner of our choosing." President Obama referred to the incident as an act of "cyber-vandalism," while others decried it as an act of cyberwar.

This incident illustrates challenges in cyberattack categorization, particularly with respect to the actors involved and their motivations as well as issues of sovereignty regarding where the actors were physically located. With the globalized nature of the Internet, perpetrators can launch cyberattacks from anywhere in the world and route the attacks through servers of third-party countries. Was the cyberattack on Sony, a private corporation with headquarters in Japan, an attack on the United States? Further, could it be considered an act of terrorism, a use of force, or cybercrime? In categorizing the attacks on Sony as an act of "cyber-vandalism," which typically includes defacing websites and is usually the realm of politically motivated actors known as "hacktivists," President Obama raised questions of what type of response could be considered "proportional," and against whom. Another potential policy question could be the circumstances under which the United States would commit troops to respond to a cyberattack. Related to this is the question of whether the US has an effective deterrence strategy in place. According to DNI Clapper, "If they get global recognition at a low cost and no consequence, they will do it again and keep doing it again until we push back."[1]

The Cyberwarfare Ecosystem: A Variety of Threat Actors

Criminals, terrorists, and spies rely heavily on cyber-based technologies to support organizational objectives. Commonly recognized cyber-aggressors and representative examples of the harm they can inflict include the following:

Cyberterrorists are state-sponsored and non-state actors who engage in cyberattacks to pursue their objectives. Transnational terrorist organizations, insurgents, and jihadists have used the Internet as a tool for planning attacks, radicalization and recruitment, a method of propaganda distribution, and a means of communication, and for disruptive purposes.[2] While no unclassified reports have been published regarding a cyberattack on a critical component of US infrastructure, the vulnerability of critical life-sustaining control systems being accessed and destroyed via the Internet has been demonstrated. In 2009, the Department of Homeland Security (DHS) conducted an experiment that revealed some of the vulnerabilities to the nation's control systems that manage power generators and grids. The experiment, known as the Aurora Project, entailed a computer-based attack on a power generator's control system that caused operations to cease and the equipment to be destroyed.[3] Cyberterrorists may be seeking a destructive capability to exploit these vulnerabilities in critical infrastructure.

Cyberspies are individuals who steal classified or proprietary information used by governments or private corporations to gain a competitive strategic, security, financial, or political advantage. These individuals often work at the behest of, and take direction from, foreign government entities. Targets include government networks, cleared defense contractors, and private companies. For example, a 2011 FBI report noted, "a company was the victim of an intrusion and had lost 10 years' worth of research and development data—valued at $1 billion—virtually overnight."[4] Likewise, in 2008 the Department of Defense's (DOD) classified computer network system was unlawfully accessed and "the computer code, placed there by a foreign intelligence agency, uploaded itself undetected onto both classified and unclassified systems from which data could be transferred to servers under foreign control."[5]

Cyberthieves are individuals who engage in illegal cyberattacks for monetary gain. Examples include an organization or individual who illegally accesses a technology system to steal and use or sell credit card numbers and someone who deceives a victim into providing access to a financial account. One estimate has placed the annual cost of cybercrime to individuals in 24 countries at $388 billion.[6] However, given the complex and sometimes ambiguous nature of the costs associated with cybercrime, and the reluctance in many cases of victims to admit to being attacked, there does not appear to be any publicly available, comprehensive, reliable assessment of the overall costs of cyberattacks.

Cyberwarriors are agents or quasi-agents of nation-states who develop capabilities and undertake cyberattacks in support of a country's strategic objectives.[7] These entities may or may not be acting on behalf of the government with respect to target selection, timing of the attack, and type(s) of cyberattack and are often blamed by the host country when accusations are levied by the nation that has been attacked. Often, when a foreign government is provided evidence that a cyberattack is emanating from its country, the nation that has been attacked is informed that the perpetrators acted of their own volition and not at the behest of the government. In August 2012 a series of cyberattacks were directed against Saudi Aramco, the world's largest oil and gas producer. The attacks compromised 30,000 computers and the code was apparently designed to disrupt or halt oil production. Some security officials have suggested that Iran may have supported this attack. However, numerous groups, some with links to nations with objectives counter to Saudi Arabia, have claimed credit for this incident.

Cyberactivists are individuals who perform cyberattacks for pleasure, philosophical, political, or other nonmonetary reasons. Examples include someone who attacks a technology system as a personal challenge (who might be termed a "classic" hacker), and a "hacktivist" such as a member of the cyber-group Anonymous who undertakes an attack for political reasons. The activities of these groups can range from nuisance-related denial of service attacks and website defacement to disrupting government and private corporation business processes.

The threats posed by these cyber-aggressors and the types of attacks they can pursue are not mutually exclusive. For example, a hacker targeting the intellectual property of a corporation may be categorized as both a cyberthief and a cyberspy. A cyberterrorist and cyberwarrior may be employing different technological capabilities in support of a nation's security and political objectives. Some reports indicate that cybercrime has now surpassed the illegal drug trade as a source of funding for terrorist groups, although there is some confusion as to whether a particular action should be categorized as cybercrime.[8] Ascertaining information about an aggressor and its capabilities and intentions is difficult.[9] The threats posed by these aggressors coupled with the United States' proclivity to be an early adopter of emerging technologies,[10] which are often interdependent and contain vulnerabilities, makes for a complex environment when considering operational responses, policies, and legislation designed to safeguard the nation's strategic economic and security interests.

[…]

Cyberterrorism

As with cyberwarfare, there is no consensus definition of what constitutes cyberterrorism. The closest in law is found in the USA PATRIOT Act 18 U.S.C. 2332b's definition of "acts of terrorism transcending national boundaries" and reference to some activities and damage defined in the Computer Fraud and Abuse Act (CFA) 18 U.S.C. 1030a-c. A notable aspect of this act is its discussion of the "punishment for an offense" entails fines or imprisonment and suggests the offending party is undertaking a criminal act rather than an act of terrorism, which some argue is an act of war if undertaken by a state actor. The CFA is written in such a manner that it could be applied to an individual or groups.

18 U.S.C. 1030(a)(1) finds it illegal for an entity to "knowingly access a computer without authorization or exceeding authorized access, and by means of such conduct having obtained information that has been determined by the United States Government pursuant to an Executive order or statute to require protection against unauthorized disclosure for reasons of national defense or foreign relations, or any restricted data...with reason to believe that such information

so obtained could be used to the injury of the United States, or to the advantage of any foreign nation." As noted in this section, it appears this statute only pertains to US government networks or networks that may contain restricted data. There is not yet a precedent for an unauthorized computer-supported intrusion rising to the level of being described as a cyberattack.

Some legal analyses define cyberterrorism as "the premeditated use of disruptive activities, or the threat thereof, against computers and/or networks, with the intention to cause harm or further social, ideological, religious, political or similar objectives, or to intimidate any person in furtherance of such objectives."[26] The USA PATRIOT Act's definition of "federal crime of terrorism" and reference to the CFA seem to follow this definition. However, these provisions are also criminal statutes and generally refer to individuals or organizations rather than state actors. Naval Post Graduate School defense analyst Dorothy Denning's definition of cyberterrorism focuses on the distinction between destructive and disruptive action.[27] Terrorism generates fear comparable to that of physical attack, and is not just a "costly nuisance."[28] Though a DDoS attack itself does not yield this kind of fear or destruction, the problem is the potential for second or third order effects. For example, if telecommunications and emergency services had been completely dismantled in a time of crisis, the effects of that sort of infrastructure attack could potentially be catastrophic. If an attack on the emergency services system had coincided with a planned real-world, kinetic event, cyberterror or even a Cyber Pearl Harbor event may be an appropriate metaphor. However in this case, the emergency service system itself is most likely not a target, but rather the result of collateral damage to a vulnerable telecommunications network.

There are a number of reasons that may explain why the term "cyberterrorism" has not been statutorily defined, including the difficulty in identifying the parameters of what should be construed applicable activities, whether articulating clear redlines would demand a response for lower-level incidents, and retaining strategic maneuverability so as not to bind future US activities in cyberspace.

[...]

Endnotes

1. See http://www.bloomberg.com/politics/articles/2015-01-07/clapper-warns-of -more-potential-north-korean-hacks- after-sony.

2. For additional information, see CRS Report RL33123, *Terrorist Capabilities for Cyberattack: Overview and Policy Issues*, by John W. Rollins and Clay Wilson.

3. See "Challenges Remain in DHS' Efforts to Security Control Systems," Department of Homeland Security, Office of Inspector General, August 2009. For a discussion of how computer code may have caused the halting of operations at an Iranian nuclear facility see CRS Report R41524, *The Stuxnet Computer Worm: Harbinger of an Emerging Warfare Capability*, by Paul K. Kerr, John W. Rollins, and Catherine A. Theohary.

4. Executive Assistant Director Shawn Henry, *Responding to the Cyber Threat*, Federal Bureau of Investigation, Baltimore, MD, 2011.

5. Department of Defense Deputy Secretary of Defense William J. Lynn III, "Defending a New Domain," *Foreign Affairs*, October 2010.

6. For discussions of federal law and issues relating to cybercrime, see CRS Report 97-1025, *Cybercrime: An Overview of the Federal Computer Fraud and Abuse Statute and Related Federal Criminal Laws*, by Charles Doyle, and CRS Report R41927, *The Interplay of Borders, Turf, Cyberspace, and Jurisdiction: Issues Confronting US Law Enforcement*, by Kristin Finklea.

7. For additional information, see CRS Report R43848, *Cyber Operations in DOD Policy and Plans: Issues for Congress*, by Catherine A. Theohary.

8. Lillian Ablon, Martin C. Libicki, Andrea A. Golay, *Markets for Cybercrime Tools and Stolen Data: Hackers' Bazaar*, RAND. For more information on cybercrime definitions, see CRS Report R42547, *Cybercrime: Conceptual Issues for Congress and US Law Enforcement*, by Kristin Finklea and Catherine A. Theohary.

9. The concept of attribution in the cyber world entails an attempt to identify with some degree of specificity and confidence the geographic location, identity, capabilities, and intention of the cyber-aggressor. Mobile technologies and sophisticated data routing processes and techniques often make attribution difficult for US intelligence and law enforcement communities.

10. Emerging cyber-based technologies that may be vulnerable to the actions of a cyber-aggressor include items that are in use but not yet widely adopted or are currently being developed. For additional information on how the convergence of inexpensive, highly sophisticated, and easily accessible technology is providing opportunities for cyber-aggressors to exploit vulnerabilities found in a technologically laden society see *Global Trends 2030: Alternative Worlds*,

National Intelligence Council, Office of the Director of National Intelligence, December 10, 2012.

26. http://www.nato.int/structur/library/bibref/cyberterrorism.pdf.

27. Dorothy E. Denning. "Activism, Hacktivism, and Cyberterrorism: The Internet as a Tool for Influencing Foreign Policy," http://www.nautilus.org/info-policy /workshop/papers/denning.html.

28. Serge Krasavin, PhD, "What Is Cyber-terrorism?" http://www.crime-research .org/library/Cyber-terrorism.htm.

There Is No Clearly Discernible Difference Between Cyberterrorism and Cyberwarfare

Aaron Wright

Aaron Wright is an Australian army education officer who is currently posted as the officer in charge of the Puckapunyal Army Education Centre. He holds a master's level graduate certificate in cybersecurity from Charles Sturt University.

The arenas in which humans seek advantages are ever changing. From land and sea to air and space, humans have found a way to contest each other and the manmade arena of cyberspace will be no exception (Tabansky, 2011, p. 79). Different actors approach cyber in unique ways depending on their goals, motivation and resources. Nation states may do strategic battle in an information war while terrorist organisations spread their message of fear through isolated cyber incidents. To further complicate matters, incidents can even be misattributed to the above, when they are in fact the work of skilled individuals for recreational fun, such as the attacks on US DOD computers systems in 1990 (Lewis, 2002, p. 8). So what differentiates warfare from terrorism? First, we shall explore two major cyber warfare doctrines, then look at two incidents and determine if they would be considered warfare or terrorism. The picture may be murkier than we believe.

Cyber Warfare

Contrasting US and Russian approaches will be effective in defining cyber warfare. The US is the sole world superpower, making it the benchmark for military competitiveness worldwide (Fritz, 2008, p. 40). The US views cyber capability, both offensively and defensively, within an effects-based approach. That is to say, it is interchangeable with a kinetic strike as the effect produced is of

"Defining Cyber Warfare and Cyber Terrorism," by Aaron Wright, The Cove, August 5, 2020. Reprinted by permission.

concern, not the means via which it is produced (Farrell & Glaser, 2017). US doctrine expresses a defensive mindset thus, "the United States military might use cyber operations to terminate an ongoing conflict on US terms, or to disrupt an adversary's military systems to prevent the use of force against US interests" (Farrell & Glaser, 2017). What does this tell us? The US (at least publicly) believes cyber warfare is an employable asset, like an aircraft, or naval fleet. A military instrument to be used at the correct time, to generate a desired result.

Russia in contrast does not even use the term cyber (*kiber*) or cyberwarfare (*kiberrvoyna*), except where referencing western doctrine, instead referring to this concept within the broader rubric of information warfare (*informatsionnaya*) (Connell & Vogler, 2017, p. 3). Instead of an act to cause an effect, it is viewed as a strategic fulcrum in the exercise of state power, both in peacetime and in wartime, to create and sustain total information dominance (Connell & Vogler, 2017, p. 6). This approach is a direct continuation of the Soviet-era Leninist doctrine of endless war (Connell & Vogler, 2017, p. 5). Thus its willingness to use cyber capability is not confined to what the West would determine "acts of war/deterrence" but rather as part of an endless doctrine of advancing Russian power.

Cyber Terrorism

The concept of cyber terrorism is young and not yet properly defined. Traditional terrorism typically has been defined as an act causing fear and harm indiscriminately (Janczewski & Colarik, 2009, p. xiv) to advance a goal. Where an act of terror ends and an act of war begins is murky at best, especially in the field of psychological warfare. Unlike its parent concept, which is constituted by serious acts of violence against people or property (Jarvis, Macdonald, Whiting, 2016, p. 36), cyber terrorism is much harder to pin down. While western organisation such as ASIO consider hacktivist groups such as Anonymous to be cyber terrorists (Joyem, 2013), others have expressed concern that what is merely private protest or dissent in the cyber space is being reclassified as cyber terrorism when it runs against the status quo or state goals (*Anonymous: Protestors or Terrorists?*, 2012). Until a clear, collective perception of what constitutes an act of cyber terrorism settles in the public subconscious, each cyber incident will need to be considered on a case by case basis, looking at the perpetrator, the goal and the impact before it could be called cyber terrorism.

Given the above discourse, it is impossible to select a "cyber warfare" and "cyber terrorism" event objectively. Instead, let us look at two significant cyber incidents, and how we would classify them.

Cyber in Practice

In late December 2015, three separate distribution centres in the Ukraine had their power grids brought offline via remote access controls, then had internal data wiped using a KillDisk malware (Connell & Vogler, 2017, p. 20). Over 220,000 Ukrainians spent six fearful hours in the dark and repairs would take months to complete. Terrorists seek to make a political statements and to inflict psychological and physical damage on their targets (Lewis, 2002, p. 8). The statement here is clear; we can take your power away when we want, with precision. Be fearful of opposing us. Is this cyber terrorism? Or do the links the pro-Russian instigators are rumoured to have, rebrand this incident as an act of cyber warfare?

The worm Win32/Stuxnet is one of the most technologically sophisticated malicious programs developed for a targeted attack to date (Matrosov, 2011). Security experts have suggested the worm was designed to specifically target Iranian Bushehr nuclear plant (Chen, 2010). Its level of sophistication and unprecedented use of four zero-day exploits suggests development by a highly competent team, almost certainly a state actor. While never proven, the use of a cyber weapon to produce a specific kinetic effect, is consistent with US effects-based cyber war doctrine, and its origin has often been believed to be American. Stuxnet more clearly falls into the category of cyber war, as there is no message being sent; instead an effect—covertly disrupting Iranian nuclear research—was the goal.

Is There a Difference?

The key takeaway is the question, do cyber acts require a recognised state actor to be considered cyber warfare instead of cyber terrorism? Or is it the intent of the act, ie, effects-based versus sending a message, that makes the difference? Acts that may be considered terrorism, such as spreading fear and uncertainty through Russia's policy of *informatsionnaya* can be considered acts of cyber war from a certain point of view. By contrast, acts that would normally be considered war if conducted under the US effects-based doctrine, become terrorism when perpetuated by an unrecognised state, such as ISIS or an independent hacker. This is further complicated by state actors who conduct covert actions against rivals and their assets using subsidiary organisations in order to achieve deniability. In the end, there may be no clear discernible difference, beyond a visceral gut reaction, between an act of cyber warfare and an act of cyber terrorism. There are only cyber incidents and the effects on society they create.

References

Chen, Thomas M. (2010). Stuxnet, the Real Start of Cyber Warfare? IEEE Network. Retrieved from https://ieeexplore.ieee.org/stamp/stamp.jsp?tp=&arnumber=5634434

Connell, Michael & Vogler, Sarah. (2017). Russia's Approach to Cyber Warfare CNA Analysis and Solutions. CNA Analysis & Solutions. Retrieved from https://www.cna.org/cna_files/pdf/DOP-2016-U-014231-1Rev.pdf

Farrell, Henry & Glaser, Charles. (2017). The Role of Effects, Saliencies and Norms in US Cyberwar Doctrine. Journal of Cybersecurity Vol 3. Retrieved from https://academic.oup.com/cybersecurity/article/3/1/7/3074707

Fritz, Jason. (2008). How China Will Use Cyber Warfare to Leapfrog in Military Competitiveness. Culture Mandala Vol 8. Retrieved from: http://www.international-relations.com/CM8-1/Cyberwar.pdf

Janczewski, Lech J. & Colarik, Andrew M. (2008). Cyber Warfare and Cyber Terrorism. New York. Hershey. Retrieved from http://citeseerx.ist.psu.edu/viewdoc/download?doi=10.1.1.670.9033&rep=rep1&type=pdf

Jarvis, Lee, Macdonald, Stuard, & Whiting, Andrew. (2016). Unpacking Cyber Terrorism Discourse: Specificty, status and scale in news media constructions of threat. Cambridge University Press. Retrieved from https://www.cambridge.org /core/journals/european-journal-of-international-security/article/unpacking -cyberterrorism-discourse-specificity-status-and-scale-in-news-media -constructions-of-threat/B68F6B8FD15E2200A5B1C159FA480210

Joyem, Cristopher. (2013). It's a Global Cyber War Out There, Financial Review. Retrieved from https://www.afr.com/policy/foreign-affairs/it-s-global-cyber-war -out-there-20130102-im8ks

Lewis, James A. (2002). Assessing the Risks of Cyber Terrorism and Other Cyber Threats. Centre for Strategic and International Studies. Retrieved from https:// www.steptoe.com/images/content/4/5/v1/4586/231a.pdf p.8

Matrosov, Aleksandr. (2011). Stuxnet Under the Microscope V 1.31. Loose Leaf. Retrieved from http://www.rpac.in/image/ITR%201.pdf

Russia Today. (2012). Anonymous: Protestors or Terrorists? Fog of cyberwar obscures truth. Retrieved from https://www.youtube.com/watch?v=W_m -1vcdzIk&feature=emb_title

Tabansky, Lior. (2011). Basic Concepts in Cyber War. Military and Strategic Affairs Vol. 3. Retrieved from http://book.itep.ru/depository/cyberwar/1308129610.pdf

CHAPTER 2

Is Cyberterrorism a Significant Threat?

Overview: Cyberattacks on Ukraine's Power Grid Show Their Potential to Do Significant Harm

Michael McElfresh

Michael McElfresh is an adjunct professor of electrical engineering at Santa Clara University, where he teaches the foundation course in the Sustainable Energy program and courses in wind power and energy storage. He is also the interim lead for power grid R&D at Argonne National Laboratory.

On December 23, 2015, two days before Christmas, the power grid in the Ivano-Frankivsk region of Ukraine went down for a reported six hours, leaving about half the homes in the region with a population of 1.4 million without power, according to the Ukrainian news media outlet TSN.

It reported that the cause of the power outage was a "hacker attack" utilizing a "virus." Outages were caused when substations—devices that route power and change voltages—were disconnected from the grid, TSN said.

There have been a handful of documented attacks on the power grid and control systems of energy systems, such as oil refineries. But this cyberattack in Ukraine counts as only the second or third to successfully derail power delivery using a software-based attack.

Because of its success, the incident has sent shock waves through cybersecurity circles. How was this attack carried out? And could something similar happen in other countries?

"Cyberattack on Ukraine Grid: Here's How It Worked and Perhaps Why It Was Done," by Michael McElfresh, The Conversation, January 18, 2016. https://theconversation.com /cyberattack-on-ukraine-grid-heres-how-it-worked-and-perhaps-why-it-was-done-52802. Licensed under CC BY-ND 4.0.

Stuxnet to BlackEnergy

Cyberattacks designed to take out the power grid have been a big concern of security specialists for many years.

Much of the concern has been focused on potential attacks on the control systems, called Supervisory Control and Data Acquisition (SCADA) systems, on which power grids are highly dependent for safe, reliable and secure operation. SCADA systems also provide critical data for operations, automation and remote control.

Some computer worms have been specifically designed to attack the types of control systems commonly found in power utilities. The most well-known is called Stuxnet, which was used to compromise Iran's uranium enrichment facilities. But a variety of similar worms have been developed that experts have feared would be used to bring down the power grid.

While the Ukraine outages were reported to involve only one utility, Prykarpattyaoblenergo, evidence of computer malware known as BlackEnergy was identified at that utility and two other regional utilities. Samples of the suspect code have since been studied, and various security companies, including iSight Partners, EBET, and SANS-ICS, have verified that it contained elements of the BlackEnergy malware.

The BlackEnergy malware is generally associated with a group referred to as Sandworm, which is believed to be based in Russia. It is not clear if Sandworm has an association with the Russian government.

Growing Sophistication

BlackEnergy started as a malware system for launching denial-of-service (DoS) attacks, which are designed to prevent legitimate users from accessing a server by any one of a number of possible mechanisms. BlackEnergy has since evolved into an effective system for data exfiltration, or the unauthorized transfer of data from a computer. Such a transfer may be manual and carried out by someone able to access the computer, or it may be automated and carried out through malicious programming placed on the computer being attacked.

About two years ago, a new version of BlackEnergy began to appear with new functions that included stealing passwords, covertly taking screenshots, gaining persistent access to command and control channels and destroying hard drives.

More recently, security software maker ESET found evidence of several new features, including a wiper component dubbed KillDisk. A wiper is software designed to erase portions of a disk and can be used to cover up evidence of an attack. In the Ukraine attack, it is not clear if BlackEnergy was used, but some of its components were present; in particular, there is evidence of KillDisk.

Some experts contend that this may not technically have been a cyberattack. The malware allowed attackers to manually intervene in the grid's operation; by contrast, the Stuxnet software inflicted damage on industrial machines.

Regardless, there was a sophisticated attack that required coordination of different types of malware, which appear to have enabled the attack.

Worries over Disabling Nuclear Plants

The Ukrainian power grid has several attributes that cause some special concern.

The bulk of the power production at any time is provided by nuclear power plants, which provide most of the steady "baseload" power to supply electricity through most of the day.

To meet fluctuations in demand—for instance, increases in power use in the morning as people begin their day—grid operators in Ukraine primarily rely on coal power plants. They do not have many avenues to import power from other countries to meet spikes and dips in demand.

This situation means that if an cyberattack causes a power outage, Ukraine grid operators may not be able to respond rapidly enough and export an excess in the flow of power, which would lead to grid instabilities and the need to shut down nuclear reactors.

There is also the issue of cooling of reactors in the event of a power outage. The cooling pumps in the nuclear reactors in Ukraine are dependent on AC power input from the grid, thereby making them susceptible in the event that backup diesel generators cannot be started.

Broader Concerns

Could this happen in the West? In short, yes. US utilities use software products from various major vendors which have been the targets of a Sandworm BlackEnergy campaign.

Thus far, there doesn't seem to have been any financial benefit from the attack. What's more, when attackers use malware, they expose their methodology, which makes it possible for security people to develop protections for that line of attack. So we have to wonder what they had to gain from the exercise.

If they have nothing to gain in the short term, like robbing banks while the grid is down, did they gain valuable experience for their next, more effective attack?

The ability to hack into a utility to throw switches (breakers) at substations, as was done in Ukraine, opens up the possibility of more serious types of attacks, as was demonstrated by the Aurora Test. In that controlled experiment, circuit breakers associated with a generator were opened and closed using software in a way that resulted in permanent damage to equipment.

While it's hard to know the attackers' intentions for sure, it appears likely that the Ukraine power grid was attacked with at least the help of the BlackEnergy malware, increasing the technological potential for disrupting power grids in general.

This incident underscores the need for diligence and the increased effort in cybersecurity that we are seeing in the government and private sectors. The continuously increasing dependence on the power grid is driving the need for cybersecurity to be part of the design of all new systems.

Cyberterrorist Attacks Can Be as Dangerous as Nuclear Attacks

Jeremy Straub

Jeremy Straub is an assistant professor of computer science at North Dakota State University. His research focuses on the relationship between technology, commercialization, and technology policy.

People around the world may be worried about nuclear tensions rising, but I think they're missing the fact that a major cyberattack could be just as damaging—and hackers are already laying the groundwork.

With the US and Russia pulling out of a key nuclear weapons pact—and beginning to develop new nuclear weapons—plus Iran tensions and North Korea again test-launching missiles, the global threat to civilization is high. Some fear a new nuclear arms race.

That threat is serious—but another could be as serious, and is less visible to the public. So far, most of the well-known hacking incidents, even those with foreign government backing, have done little more than steal data. Unfortunately, there are signs that hackers have placed malicious software inside US power and water systems, where it's lying in wait, ready to be triggered. The US military has also reportedly penetrated the computers that control Russian electrical systems.

Many Intrusions Already

As someone who studies cybersecurity and information warfare, I'm concerned that a cyberattack with widespread impact, an intrusion in one area that spreads to others or a combination of lots of smaller attacks, could cause significant damage, including mass injury and death rivaling the death toll of a nuclear weapon.

"A Cyberattack Could Wreak Destruction Comparable to a Nuclear Weapon," by Jeremy Straub, The Conversation, August 16, 2019. https://theconversation.com/a-cyberattack -could-wreak-destruction-comparable-to-a-nuclear-weapon-112173. Licensed under CC BY-ND 4.0.

Unlike a nuclear weapon, which would vaporize people within 100 feet and kill almost everyone within a half-mile, the death toll from most cyberattacks would be slower. People might die from a lack of food, power or gas for heat or from car crashes resulting from a corrupted traffic light system. This could happen over a wide area, resulting in mass injury and even deaths.

This might sound alarmist, but look at what has been happening in recent years, in the US and around the world.

In early 2016, hackers took control of a US treatment plant for drinking water, and changed the chemical mixture used to purify the water. If changes had been made—and gone unnoticed—this could have led to poisonings, an unusable water supply and a lack of water.

In 2016 and 2017, hackers shut down major sections of the power grid in Ukraine. This attack was milder than it could have been, as no equipment was destroyed during it, despite the ability to do so. Officials think it was designed to send a message. In 2018, unknown cybercriminals gained access throughout the United Kingdom's electricity system; in 2019 a similar incursion may have penetrated the US grid.

In August 2017, a Saudi Arabian petrochemical plant was hit by hackers who tried to blow up equipment by taking control of the same types of electronics used in industrial facilities of all kinds throughout the world. Just a few months later, hackers shut down monitoring systems for oil and gas pipelines across the US. This primarily caused logistical problems—but it showed how an insecure contractor's systems could potentially cause problems for primary ones.

The FBI has even warned that hackers are targeting nuclear facilities. A compromised nuclear facility could result in the discharge of radioactive material, chemicals or even possibly a reactor meltdown. A cyberattack could cause an event similar to the incident in Chernobyl. That explosion, caused by inadvertent error, resulted in 50 deaths and evacuation of 120,000 and has left parts of the region uninhabitable for thousands of years into the future.

Mutual Assured Destruction

My concern is not intended to downplay the devastating and immediate effects of a nuclear attack. Rather, it's to point out that some of the international protections against nuclear conflicts don't exist for cyberattacks. For instance, the idea of "mutual assured destruction" suggests that no country should launch a nuclear weapon at another nuclear-armed nation: The launch would likely be detected, and the target nation would launch its own weapons in response, destroying both nations.

Cyberattackers have fewer inhibitions. For one thing, it's much easier to disguise the source of a digital incursion than it is to hide where a missile blasted off from. Further, cyberwarfare can start small, targeting even a single phone or laptop. Larger attacks might target businesses, such as banks or hotels, or a government agency. But those aren't enough to escalate a conflict to the nuclear scale.

Nuclear Grade Cyberattacks

There are three basic scenarios for how a nuclear grade cyberattack might develop. It could start modestly, with one country's intelligence service stealing, deleting or compromising another nation's military data. Successive rounds of retaliation could expand the scope of the attacks and the severity of the damage to civilian life.

In another situation, a nation or a terrorist organization could unleash a massively destructive cyberattack—targeting several electricity utilities, water treatment facilities or industrial plants at once, or in combination with each other to compound the damage.

Perhaps the most concerning possibility, though, is that it might happen by mistake. On several occasions, human and mechanical errors very nearly destroyed the world during the Cold War; something analogous could happen in the software and hardware of the digital realm.

Defending Against Disaster

Just as there is no way to completely protect against a nuclear attack, there are only ways to make devastating cyberattacks less likely.

The first is that governments, businesses and regular people need to secure their systems to prevent outside intruders from finding their way in, and then exploiting their connections and access to dive deeper.

Critical systems, like those at public utilities, transportation companies and firms that use hazardous chemicals, need to be much more secure. One analysis found that only about one-fifth of companies that use computers to control industrial machinery in the US even monitor their equipment to detect potential attacks—and that in 40% of the attacks they did catch, the intruder had been accessing the system for more than a year. Another survey found that nearly three-quarters of energy companies had experienced some sort of network intrusion in the previous year.

But all those systems can't be protected without skilled cybersecurity staffs to handle the work. At present, nearly a quarter of all cybersecurity jobs in the US are vacant, with more positions opening up than there are people to fill them. One recruiter has expressed concern that even some of the jobs that are filled are held by people who aren't qualified to do them. The solution is more training and education, to teach people the skills they need to do cybersecurity work, and to keep existing workers up to date on the latest threats and defense strategies.

If the world is to hold off major cyberattacks—including some with the potential to be as damaging as a nuclear strike—it will be up to each person, each company, each government agency to work on its own and together to secure the vital systems on which people's lives depend.

Terrorist Organizations Are Recruiting Hackers with the Potential to Make Dangerous Attacks

Emma Graham-Harrison

Emma Graham-Harrison is an international affairs correspondent for the Guardian *and the* Observer. *She is currently based in London.*

When a chubby Birmingham teenager went on trial in 2012 for hacking Tony Blair's personal address book, and taking down an anti-terror hotline, defence lawyers described him as "shy and unassuming" and dismissed the online exploits as a childish prank.

"They weren't terrorists in any way, shape or form," his barrister argued in court. Less than two years later, Junaid Hussain was in Syria, apparently on his way to join Isis, one of its most dangerous new recruits.

The group transfixed the world with its ultraviolent ideology, as it swept through Syria and Iraq in a frenzy of bloodshed and destruction. But its leaders' enthusiasm for medieval barbarity is matched by an equally fervent embrace of modern technology. They know that a hacker like Hussain, behind his laptop, is as intimidating to some of their distant enemies as the gunmen terrorising people on the ground.

"Isis has been recruiting hackers for some time now. Some are virtual collaborators from a distance, but others have been recruited to emigrate to Syria," said JM Berger, co-author of *Isis: The State of Terror*. "Activity targeting the west is just part of their portfolio. They're also responsible for maintaining internet access in Isis territories, for instance, and for instructing members on security."

"Could Isis's 'Cyber Caliphate' Unleash a Deadly Attack on Key Targets?" by Emma Graham-Harrison, Guardian News and Media Limited, April 12, 2015. Reprinted by permission.

The group's skill at manipulating social media, for recruitment and projection of power, has been acknowledged even by enemies and rivals, who have poured resources into trying to dismantle, defuse—or in the case of other jihadi groups, emulate—its online success.

Perhaps its most dramatic publicity coup came in January, when the Twitter and YouTube accounts of the US Central Military Command (Centcom) were hacked by a group calling itself the "CyberCaliphate." Intelligence experts suspect Hussain was the mastermind.

The hackers scrawled "I love you Isis" across the page and sent out tweets including pictures showing US personnel in a command outpost and military documents, suggesting Isis sympathisers had somehow infiltrated military servers and installations.

In fact, although the attack was deeply embarrassing, it was more like the digital equivalent of graffiti in an entrance hall than a theft of sensitive files from the Pentagon. The information shared was widely available and non-official, and Central Command said that no classified information was divulged or operational networks affected, and it viewed the hack as "purely an act of vandalism."

That reflects a wider online strategy apparently focused more on publicity than damage so far, but internet security experts and analysts who have studied the rise of Isis warn that its enemies should not be complacent about its capacities or intent.

"They have not yet been extremely visible carrying out more sophisticated activities such as high-level cybercrime or more destructive attacks, but I suspect this is just a matter of time," Berger said. "This is a very low-cost way to publicise their cause and harass their enemies."

None of the risks posed by Isis is unique to the group. They are part of a fast-growing vulnerability as we rush headlong to put our lives and our businesses online, and our security and justice systems struggle to keep up. There have always been connections between criminal and terrorist networks and the online world is no different.

But the dangers posed by Isis may be more acute because of its embrace of modern technology, mastery of the difficult art of online propaganda and its appeal to young, computer-literate foreigners, including known hackers.

What rival organisations can only dream of attempting in a distant future, Raqqa's rulers may be able to pursue now. Skilled recruits like Hussain can reach into our increasingly interconnected western cities and potentially bring them to a standstill, just as effectively as sympathisers armed with knives and guns have done over the last year.

"We have seen many politically motivated hackings in recent years, emanating from terrorist and militant groups, or on their behalf ... and, so far, the damage they have done has mainly caused inconveniences rather than serious damage," said Professor Gabriella Blum, author of *The Future of Violence: Robots and Germs, Hackers and Drones*. "Why haven't we seen more or worse? Is it a matter of lack of capability, a lack of motivation, or just constricted imagination? Probably a combination of the three. But at least the first factor—capability and access to materials and knowhow—is growing rapidly. This is bound to affect the incidence and magnitude of attacks that will utilise new technologies."

Hacking attacks on our basic infrastructure may seem the stuff of sci-fi nightmare, interconnected cities held hostage to a malign genius. But it is already reality, security expert Marc Goodman argues in his book *Future Crimes*, where he details a string of such attacks. A Brazilian power station shuttered by mafia hackers after their demands for protection money were not met, a Polish tram derailed by a bored teenager, and in Australia the sluice gates of a sewage station opened to pour waste over fields and parks—all masterminded by people behind screens.

Attackers often share their success or what they have learned from failure, raising future vulnerability to other hackers, regardless of their affiliation. "One well-known hacker database, Shodan, provides tips on how to exploit everything from power plants to wind turbines," Goodman writes. "It is searchable by country, company or device, providing detailed how-tos and greatly lowering the technical bar and knowledge for any rogue individual to hack our critical infrastructures."

Vulnerability only gets worse as the world goes further online, with an "internet of things" designed for convenience that could also be used for intelligence gathering and attacks. Smartphones and TVs can already be turned into microphones that listen in on their owners. Facebook even promotes digital eavesdropping as a useful feature, for subscribers who want friends to automatically know what music they are listening to, or what programmes they are watching.

More dangerous everyday items have become hackable too, including cars. "Security researchers have proven it is entirely possible for criminals 1,500 miles away to seize control of your car when you are driving 65mph down the highway," Goodman writes. "What they do with your hacked vehicle is limited only by their imaginations."

Britain's new spy chief warned last month that the country was now in a "technology arms race" with enemies "often unconstrained by consideration of ethics and law ... terrorists, malicious actors in cyberspace and criminals." "[The technology] allows them to see what we are doing and to put our people and agents at risk," Alex Younger told an audience in London, adding that traditional human espionage was becoming increasingly intertwined with "technical operations."

For now, a key deterrent to planning a spectacular hacking attack coordinated out of Raqqa may be a simple question of resources, as Isis deals with heavy military pressure on the ground, according to Hassan Hassan, analyst and author of *Isis: Inside the Army of Terror*. His book details the group's technical agility at exploiting everything from the Zello app, which turns phones into walkie-talkies, to drones, to the hackers they tempted to Syria.

"Isis targets this kind of people [hackers], tries to recruit them … but maybe it is not their priority at the moment," he said. "They did the attack on Centcom, and when they were in full control of their territory in Iraq and Syria, they were using drones and other things, but now they are focused on military operations."

Isis is now battling to hold territory under assault from a motley coalition including the US, Iran and conventional Iraqi forces.

An online offensive may also be distracting members of the "cyber caliphate." Western governments, the companies whose social media platforms they use and even some fellow hackers, from the Anonymous collective, have declared war on their internet presence. After months of rampaging through cyberspace as they swept through Iraq and Syria, the members are now lamenting the "devastating" impact of these efforts to shut down their propaganda machine, Berger says.

Even without the distractions of a game of online cat and mouse, Isis hackers would likely find attacking a specific physical target more challenging than the propaganda hits that have been their focus so far, security experts say, because they require more time and skills.

Perhaps the most famous and dramatic cyber-attack the world has seen so far was the stuxnet worm, a virus that went unnoticed for years, and baffled experts even after it was found. Eventually it became clear that it was a meticulously designed program with just one aim, knocking out the centrifuges at Iran's nuclear enrichment plant.

It took a large team months, perhaps years, of work to develop both the sophisticated coding and the social engineering needed to get the virus into a system not connected to the internet. Once in place, it took years to have full effect.

Stuxnet is an extreme example, because it targeted what was probably one of the most heavily guarded systems in the world. But almost all institutions now have some form of digital security, and its creation underlines the patience usually needed to go after a physical target.

"If you are talking about defacing a website probably one person could do that," said David Emm, principal security researcher at the Kaspersky lab. "If you want to get more serious and talk about infiltrating an organisation you probably need some more people to do the research—who works there, what are their email addresses, what are their interests. It's typically going to mean exploiting a human weakness, framing an email to them that is going to make them click [on something containing malware], so there is more legwork, if only because of the intelligence."

Once inside any system, the hacking itself would also be much more challenging. Most commercial attacks involve effectively sneaking into a system to gather sensitive information unnoticed, while an attempt to sabotage infrastructure would be far more likely to set off digital alarms.

"If on the other hand you don't just want to blend in and gather information, you want to subvert a physical process, you have much more work to do to mask your presence," Emm said.

The relative ease of hacking for cash rather than for sabotage might tempt Isis hackers to focus on that instead, especially as the group is reportedly struggling with the expensive business of trying to run a state.

Last year its coffers were flush with cash from oil wells, looting and hostage ransoms, but the oil price has crashed, the rapid expansion that made looting so profitable has slowed, and the captives are mostly dead or gone now.

There is a template for using online robbery to fund real-world attacks. Mobile phone fraud helped pay for the 2004 Madrid train bombings, Goodman says, and the terrorist group that attacked Mumbai in 2008 got $2m from a hacking gang in the Philippines, routed through intermediaries in the Gulf. The money can be extremely hard to trace, once it has been skimmed from bank accounts, phones or other online transactions. Even for supporters based outside Isis territory, the risks are fairly low; the chance of ending up in court is only around 0.01%, Goodman says.

Still, Isis has drawn in elite hackers, a group that often thrives on a challenge. The risk they might venture beyond propaganda or cyber-theft to substantive attacks on cities and infrastructure may be small, but it is certainly real. Far too little is being done to analyse and prepare for the threat, by governments or the companies that run our power and our water, our transport, our banks.

"The quality of protection is always measured in outcomes: the fact that so far, we haven't suffered major harms is reassuring," Blum said. "If, however, you believe that the frequency and ease with which these attacks are conducted is a trend that is likely to grow worse in the future … there isn't enough protection."

Iran's Military Hires Hackers for Cyberattacks

Dorothy E. Denning

Dorothy E. Denning is an American information security researcher and a distinguished professor emeritus of defense analysis at the Naval Postgraduate School. She served as the first president of the International Association for Cryptologic Research and has testified before the US Congress on encryption policy and cyberterrorism.

In the wake of the US killing of a top Iranian general and Iran's retaliatory missile strike, should the US be concerned about the cyberthreat from Iran? Already, pro-Iranian hackers have defaced several US websites to protest the killing of General Qassem Soleimani. One group wrote "This is only a small part of Iran's cyber capability" on one of the hacked sites.

Two years ago, I wrote that Iran's cyberwarfare capabilities lagged behind those of both Russia and China, but that it had become a major threat which will only get worse. It had already conducted several highly damaging cyberattacks.

Since then, Iran has continued to develop and deploy its cyberattacking capabilities. It carries out attacks through a network of intermediaries, allowing the regime to strike its foes while denying direct involvement.

Islamic Revolutionary Guard Corps–Supported Hackers

Iran's cyberwarfare capability lies primarily within Iran's Islamic Revolutionary Guard Corps, a branch of the country's military. However, rather than employing its own cyberforce against foreign targets, the Islamic Revolutionary Guard Corps appears to mainly outsource these cyberattacks.

"How Iran's Military Outsources Its Cyberthreat Forces," by Dorothy E. Denning, The Conversation, January 22, 2020. https://theconversation.com/how-irans-military -outsources-its-cyberthreat-forces-129536. Licensed under CC BY-ND 4.0.

According to cyberthreat intelligence firm Recorded Future, the Islamic Revolutionary Guard Corps uses trusted intermediaries to manage contracts with independent groups. These intermediaries are loyal to the regime but separate from it. They translate the Iranian military's priorities into discrete tasks, which are then bid out to independent contractors.

Recorded Future estimates that as many as 50 organizations compete for these contracts. Several contractors may be involved in a single operation.

Iranian contractors communicate online to hire workers and exchange information. Ashiyane, the primary online security forum in Iran, was created by hackers in the mid-2000s in order to disseminate hacking tools and tutorials within the hacking community. The Ashiyane Digital Security Team was known for hacking websites and replacing their home pages with pro-Iranian content. By May 2011, Zone-H, an archive of defaced websites, had recorded 23,532 defacements by that group alone. Its leader, Behrouz Kamalian, said his group cooperated with the Iranian military, but operated independently and spontaneously.

Iran had an active community of hackers at least by 2004, when a group calling itself Iran Hackers Sabotage launched a succession of web attacks "with the aim of showing the world that Iranian hackers have something to say in the worldwide security." It is likely that many of Iran's cyber contractors come from this community.

Iran's use of intermediaries and contractors makes it harder to attribute cyberattacks to the regime. Nevertheless, investigators have been able to trace many cyberattacks to persons inside Iran operating with the support of the country's Islamic Revolutionary Guard Corps.

Cyber Campaigns

Iran engages in both espionage and sabotage operations. They employ both off-the-shelf malware and custom-made software tools, according to a 2018 report by the Foundation to Defend Democracy. They use spearfishing, or luring specific individuals with fraudulent messages, to gain initial access to target machines by enticing victims to click on links that lead to phony sites where they hand over usernames and passwords or open attachments that plant "backdoors" on their devices. Once in, they use various hacking tools to spread through networks and download or destroy data.

Iran's cyber espionage campaigns gain access to networks in order to steal proprietary and sensitive data in areas of interest to the regime. Security companies that track these threats give them APT (Advanced Persistent Threat) names such as APT33, "kitten" names such as Magic Kitten and miscellaneous other names such as OilRig.

The group the security firm FireEye calls APT33 is especially noteworthy. It has conducted numerous espionage operations against oil and aviation industries in the US, Saudi Arabia and elsewhere. APT33 was recently reported to use small botnets (networks of compromised computers) to target very specific sites for their data collection.

Another group known as APT35 (aka Phosphoros) has attempted to gain access to email accounts belonging to individuals involved in a 2020 US presidential campaign. Were they to succeed, they might be able to use stolen information to influence the election by, for example, releasing information publicly that could be damaging to a candidate.

In 2018, the US Department of Justice charged nine Iranians with conducting a massive cyber theft campaign on behalf of the Islamic Revolutionary Guard Corps. All were tied to the Mabna Institute, an Iranian company behind cyber intrusions since at least 2013. The defendants allegedly stole 31 terabytes of data from US and foreign entities. The victims included over 300 universities, almost 50 companies and several government agencies.

Cyber Sabotage

Iran's sabotage operations have employed "wiper" malware to destroy data on hard drives. They have also employed botnets to launch distributed denial-of-service attacks, where a flood of traffic effectively disables a server. These operations are frequently hidden behind monikers that resemble those used by independent hacktivists who hack for a cause rather than money.

In one highly damaging attack, a group calling themselves the Cutting Sword of Justice attacked the Saudi Aramco oil company with wiper code in 2012. The hackers used a virus dubbed Shamoon to spread the code through the company's network. The attack destroyed data on 35,000 computers, disrupting business processes for weeks.

The Shamoon software reappeared in 2016, wiping data from thousands of computers in Saudi Arabia's civil aviation agency and other organizations. Then in 2018, a variant of Shamoon hit the Italian oil services firm Saipem, crippling more than 300 computers.

Iranian hackers have conducted massive distributed denial-of-service attacks. From 2012 to 2013, a group calling itself the Cyber Fighters of Izz ad-Din al-Qassam launched a series of relentless distributed denial-of-service attacks against major US banks. The attacks were said to have caused tens of millions of dollars in losses relating to mitigation and recovery costs and lost business.

In 2016 the US indicted seven Iranian hackers for working on behalf of the Islamic Revolutionary Guard Corps to conduct the bank attacks. The motivation may have been retaliation for economic sanctions that had been imposed on Iran.

Looking Ahead

So far, Iranian cyberattacks have been limited to desktop computers and servers running standard commercial software. They have not yet affected industrial controls systems running electrical power grids and other physical infrastructure. Were they to get into and take over these control systems, they could, for example, cause more serious damage such as the 2015 and 2016 power outages caused by the Russians in Ukraine.

One of the Iranians indicted in the bank attacks did get into the computer control system for the Bowman Avenue Dam in rural

New York. According to the indictment, no damage was done, but the access would have allowed the dam's gate to be manipulated if it not been manually disconnected for maintenance issues.

While there are no public reports of Iranian threat actors demonstrating a capability against industrial control systems, Microsoft recently reported that APT33 appears to have shifted its focus to these systems. In particular, they have been attempting to guess passwords for the systems' manufacturers, suppliers, and maintainers. The access and information that could be acquired from succeeding might help them get into an industrial control system.

Ned Moran, a security researcher with Microsoft, speculated that the group may be attempting to get access to industrial control systems in order to produce physically disruptive effects. Although APT33 has not been directly implicated in any incidents of cyber sabotage, security researchers have found links between code used by the group with code used in the Shamoon attacks to destroy data.

While it is impossible to know Iran's intentions, they are likely to continue operating numerous cyber espionage campaigns while developing additional capabilities for cyber sabotage. If tensions between Iran and the United States mount, Iran may respond with additional cyberattacks, possibly ones that are more damaging than we've seen so far.

Terrorists Use the Internet to Organize and Manipulate Public Opinion, Not to Attack

Irving Lachow and Courtney Richardson

Irving Lachow is a senior researcher at National Defense University and the research director of the Center for Information Assurance Education in Washington, DC. Courtney Richardson served as a research assistant at the Center for Technology and National Security Policy at National Defense University.

*C*yberterrorism conjures images of infrastructure failures, economic disasters, and even large-scale loss of life. It also receives a great deal of coverage in the press. While the threat of cyberterrorism is real, the hype surrounding the issue often outpaces the magnitude of the threat. In addition, the term itself deflects attention from a more mundane but equally serious problem: terrorist organizations effectively using the Internet to stymie US efforts to win the Long War.

The Internet enables terrorist groups to operate as either highly decentralized franchises or freelancers. Similar to information age businesses, these groups use the Internet to create a brand image, market themselves, recruit followers, raise capital, identify partners and suppliers, provide training materials, and even manage operations. As a result, these groups have become more numerous, agile, and well coordinated, all of which make them harder to stop.[1] Furthermore, these groups have become expert at using the Internet to manipulate both public opinion and media coverage in ways that undermine American interests. In short, rather than *attacking* the Internet, terrorists are *using* it to survive and thrive.

This article examines why the Internet is so useful for terrorist organizations. It then considers how terrorists use the Internet for strategic advantage and why the threat of cyberterrorism may

"Terrorist Use of the Internet: The Real Story," by Irving Lachow and Courtney Richardson, National Defense University Press. Reprinted by permission.

be overstated in many cases. The article concludes with a set of observations and recommendations.

[...]

Cyberterrorism?

It is evident that terrorist groups are extremely effective in using the Internet to further their missions. Are they also using, or planning to use, the Internet to launch a major cyber attack on the United States? We do not know, but there are a number of factors that suggest the answer to this question is no. Terrorism, by definition, is focused on obtaining desired political or social outcomes through the use of tactics that instill fear and horror in target populations. *Cyberterror* can be defined as:

> a computer based attack or threat of attack intended to intimidate or coerce governments or societies in pursuit of goals that are political, religious, or ideological. The attack should be sufficiently destructive or disruptive to generate fear comparable to that from physical acts of terrorism. Attacks that lead to death or bodily injury, extended power outages, plane crashes, water contamination, or major economic losses would be examples. ... Attacks that disrupt nonessential services or that are mainly a costly nuisance would not.[8]

History shows that the vast majority of cyber attacks, even viruses that cause billions of dollars of damage to an economy, are not going to cause the levels of fear desired by most terrorists. In comparison, using physical means to create terror is fairly easy and quite effective. Put in these terms, it is not surprising that terrorists prefer to inflict damage with physical means and then use the Internet to magnify the results of their handiwork. Indeed, while there is clear evidence that terrorists have used the Internet to gather intelligence and coordinate efforts to launch physical attacks against various infrastructure targets, there has not been a single documented incidence of cyberterrorism against the US Government.[9]

One could argue that terrorists would use the Internet to attack cyber assets that control physical systems, thereby creating horrific physical effects via cyber means. The most likely scenario of this type is an attack on the control systems that manage parts of the nation's infrastructure (for example, dams, trains, and powerplants). The consequences of an attack of this kind would be serious, so this threat deserves attention. However, the actual *likelihood* of such an attack is unknown; different analyses have reached different conclusions.[10]

Two things are certain: successfully launching such an attack would not be easy, and the consequences are difficult to predict due to the incredible complexity and interdependence of critical infrastructures. Given a choice of conducting either a cyber attack whose consequences are unknown (and which may not have the desired effect even if it does work) or a physical attack that is almost certain to cause graphic deaths that will create fear, it is understandable why terrorists have (so far) chosen the latter.

Observations

Terrorists use the Internet to harm US national security, but *not* by attacking infrastructure or military assets directly. Instead, terrorists use the Internet to improve their operational effectiveness while simultaneously undermining our military and diplomatic efforts to win the war of ideas. There is little doubt that they are doing both things well. While there is a possibility that they may use the Internet to launch a cyberterror attack against American targets, this threat falls under the broad umbrella of critical infrastructure protection—a topic that is getting a great deal of attention at all levels of government.[11] This issue is not addressed here. Rather, the focus rests on the other two uses of the Internet—issues that are equally important but often receive comparatively less focus, energy, and resources.

Terrorist Operational Effectiveness

The Internet enables terrorist organizations to operate as virtual transnational organizations. They can use it to raise funds, recruit, train, command and control, gather intelligence, and share information. Clearly, it is in the US interest to either disrupt or undermine these activities. The good news is that relying on the Internet is a double-edged sword for terrorist organizations: despite the many benefits associated with using the Internet as their main intelligence, command and control, and communications system, this approach carries a few liabilities. Terrorist reliance on Web sites and discussion forums allows outsiders to monitor their methods and track trends. For example, there are groups such as the SITE Institute that focus on monitoring terrorist Web sites and providing information to a wide range of interested parties, including elements within the US Government.[12] Reliance on the Internet also creates the opportunity for outsiders to pose as insiders in order to provide misinformation or simply to create doubt among the terrorists about whom they can trust.

To that end, the United States should make every effort to infiltrate extremist virtual communities in order to gather intelligence and begin planting the seeds of mistrust that can disable terrorist cells. We presume that governmental activities of this kind are under way. Surprisingly, nongovernmental organizations appear to contribute to these efforts as well. For example, individual citizens have infiltrated terrorist networks via chat rooms and then worked with governmental agencies to bring about several arrests.[13]

The bad news is that terrorists are doing their best to minimize the liabilities associated with heavy reliance on the Internet. They are quick to learn from mistakes and to disseminate best practices on how to defeat the tactics used by intelligence and law enforcement agencies.[14] Terrorist groups are adept at quickly moving their Web sites from host to host, which makes them difficult to track and shut down (trusted members of these groups use chat rooms, email, and other forums to share information about the new location of a moved site). They also like to masquerade some activities as legitimate business operations.

Terrorist Influence Operations

One of the most difficult challenges facing the United States is countering terrorist use of the Internet to propagate their ideological agenda. This problem is part of the much broader war of ideas against the extremist Islamic movement. Efforts to date have not proven successful, as evidenced by the following statement from former Secretary of Defense Donald Rumsfeld: "If I were grading I would say we probably deserve a 'D' or a 'D-plus' as a country as to how well we're doing in the battle of ideas that's taking place in the world today."[15] This is a complex issue that does not lend itself to easy answers.

Recommendations

US efforts to influence must be tied to real-world actions. While it is easy to focus on the principles of effective communications strategies, our words will ring hollow if they are not related to the realities experienced by the target audience. Thus, it goes without saying that what the United States does is as important, if not more so, as what it says. To that end, diplomatic and military influence operations must ensure that target audiences are aware of the positive actions undertaken by the United States in the Muslim world, while simultaneously highlighting the negative actions of our enemies.

The corollary to this point is that the United States must effectively get its story out before the terrorists or insurgents can use the Internet to spin events in their favor. It is much harder to respond to or discredit initial stories, even ones that are untrue, than to establish the baseline facts or perceptions in the first place. There are certainly elements of the US Government making heroic efforts in this area. For example, the Department of State maintains a Web site in a number of languages (including Arabic, Farsi, and French) that is devoted to countering false stories that appear in extremist sources. It also focuses on countering disinformation likely to end up in the mainstream media. US Embassies have used this resource to counter disinformation in extremist print publications in Pakistan and elsewhere. There are also military units deployed overseas that are exhibiting best practices in operational level influence operations.[16] Unfortunately, much work remains to be done for such examples to become the rule rather than the exception.

A related point is that the nation must view the war of ideas as equal in importance to the military and law enforcement aspects of the war on terror. The war-of-ideas aspect of any decision involving the Long War must be considered at the highest levels of US policymaking. That emphasis must then be communicated down the chain so that all players understand the importance of *message* in this war. Strategic communications cannot be seen as an afterthought of a military operation or as the sole responsibility of an office buried within the State Department. The recent announcement that the Office of the Secretary of Defense is creating a new office focused on strategic communications is a move in the right direction. Similarly, information operations cannot be viewed simply as a set of activities done by a local commander in support of tactical objectives. It is clear from past experience that such approaches are not effective in the long run if they are not tied to strategic considerations.

Countering terrorist use of the Internet to further ideological agendas will require a strategic, government-wide (interagency) approach to designing and implementing policies to win the war of ideas. For example, to counter terrorist influence operations, all Federal agencies should use the same specific and accurate language when referring to Salafist extremists. It is of the utmost importance that American policymakers set their terms of the debate. Expressions such as *jihad* and *mujahideen* are part of the popular lexicon describing antiterrorist operations in Iraq, Afghanistan, and elsewhere. However, such terms disempower the United States. Jihad literally means "striving" and is frequently used to describe every Muslim's responsibility to strive in the path of God. Mujahideen is closely translated to mean "holy warriors." Such a term may have worked to US advantage in Afghanistan against the Soviet Union—however, terms such as these now pit the United States as the enemy against holy warriors in a holy war. Rather, terms such as *hirabah* ("unholy war") and *irhabists* ("terrorists") should become part of the popular lexicon.[17]

As important as it is for the United States to improve its own communications efforts, a key part of countering extremist misinformation and propaganda is to have messages come from a variety of sources—preferably some of them local. For example, it is critical for the United States to promote the views of well-respected Muslim clerics, who counter the claims made by Islamic terrorists and extremists. Such efforts have been undertaken by the government of Saudi Arabia, but American efforts in this area have been lacking.[18] In effect, the Nation should do everything possible to enable moderate Muslims to develop a strong, vibrant, and responsive Internet and media presence of their own.

Last but not least, resources must be made available to support all of these efforts, plus others that are not mentioned here but are equally important, such as training and education to improve understanding of Muslim cultures and languages spoken within these cultures. Current US resources dedicated to strategic communications, public diplomacy, and information operations are woefully inadequate.[19] On the military side, the lack of training and education in information operations at all levels—strategic, operational, and tactical—often requires commanders to learn on the job and build information operations teams "out of hide."[20] While some leaders will certainly rise to the occasion, this approach is not a recipe for success in a complex, media-heavy war against adversaries who are highly adept at conducting their own influence operations.

Terrorists use the Internet to harm US national security interests, but not by conducting large-scale cyber attacks. Instead, they use the Internet to boost their relative power to plan and conduct physical attacks, spread their ideology, manipulate the public and media, recruit and train new terrorists, raise funds, gather information on potential targets, and control operations. If these activities can be curtailed, then the viability of the terrorist groups themselves may be put into question. To that end, the United States needs to focus more resources into two areas: countering the operational effectiveness associated with terrorist use of the Internet, and undermining Internet-based terrorist influence operations. If it can successfully meet these two challenges, the United States will make significant progress toward winning the Long War.

Notes

1. See Statement of Henry A. Crumpton, Coordinator for Counterterrorism, Department of State, Committee on Senate Foreign Relations, June 13, 2006.

8. Dorothy E. Denning, "Is Cyber Terror Next?" in *Understanding September 11*, ed. Craig Calhoun, Paul Price, and Ashley Timmer (New York: The New Press, 2002), 193.

9. Evidence of the former is cited in Stephen Ulph, "Internet Mujahideen Intensify Research on US Economic Targets," *Terrorism Focus* 3, no. 2 (January 18, 2006). The latter observation comes from several sources, including Weimann, 149; and Joshua Green, "The Myth of Cyber-Terrorism," *Washington Monthly*, November 2002, available at <www.washingtonmonthly.com /features/2001/0211.green.html>.

10. For differing perspectives on this issue, see James Lewis, "Cyber Terror: Missing in Action," *Knowledge, Technology & Policy* 16, no. 2 (Summer 2003), 34–41; and Dan Verton, *Black-Ice: The Invisible Threat of Cyber-Terrorism* (New York: McGraw-Hill/Osborne, 2003).

11. See, for example, The White House, *The National Strategy to Secure Cyberspace*, February 2003; and Department of Homeland Security, *National Infrastructure Protection Plan*, 2006.

12. See Benjamin Wallace-Wells, "Private Jihad," *The New Yorker*, May 29, 2006.

13. For example, see Blaine Harden, "In Montana, Casting a Web for Terrorists," *The Washington Post*, June 4, 2006, A3.

14. For example, see Abdul Hameed Bakier, "The Evolution of Jihadi Electronic Counter-Measures," *Terrorism Monitor* 4, no. 17 (September 8, 2006).

15. See <www.cbsnews.com/stories/2006/03/27/terror/main1442811.shtml>.

16. An excellent example is found in Colonel Ralph O. Baker, USA, "The Decisive Weapon: A Brigade Combat Team Commander's Perspective on Information Operations," *Military Review* (May–June 2006), 13–32. This article should

be required reading for everyone in the US Government remotely involved in the Long War, and especially for Active duty forces heading to Iraq and Afghanistan.

17. For more detail, see Douglas E. Streusand and Harry C. Tunnell, "Choosing Words Carefully: Language to Help Fight Islamic Terrorism," Center for Strategic Communications, National Defense University, available at <www.ndu.edu/csc/products.cfm>; and Jim Guirard, "Hirabah versus Jihad: Rescuing Jihad from the al Qaeda Blasphemy," *The American Muslim*, July 6, 2003, available at <http://theamericanmuslim.org/tam.php/features/articles/terrorism_hirabah_versus_jihad_rescuing_jihad_from_the_al_qaeda_blasphemy/>.

18. For more details, see Robert Spencer, "Losing the War of Ideas," FrontPageMagazine.com, February 5, 2004.

19. See, for example, Office of the Under Secretary of Defense for Acquisition, Technology, and Logistics, *Report of the Defense Science Board Task Force on Strategic Communication* (Washington, DC: Department of Defense, September 2004).

20. Baker, 20.

The Threat of Cyberterrorism Has Been Overblown by the Government and the Media

Gabriel Weimann

Gabriel Weimann is a professor of communications at the University of Haifa in Israel and a former fellow at the Woodrow Wilson International Center for Scholars, a highly recognized think tank. He began researching terrorist websites in the 1990s and since then has published over 180 papers and reports on the topic.

The threat posed by cyberterrorism has grabbed the attention of the mass media, the security community, and the information technology (IT) industry. Journalists, politicians, and experts in a variety of fields have popularized a scenario in which sophisticated cyberterrorists electronically break into computers that control dams or air traffic control systems, wreaking havoc and endangering not only millions of lives but national security itself. And yet, despite all the gloomy predictions of a cyber-generated doomsday, no single instance of real cyberterrorism has been recorded.

Just how real is the threat that cyberterrorism poses? Because most critical infrastructure in Western societies is networked through computers, the potential threat from cyberterrorism is, to be sure, very alarming. Hackers, although not motivated by the same goals that inspire terrorists, have demonstrated that individuals can gain access to sensitive information and to the operation of crucial services. Terrorists, at least in theory, could thus follow the hackers' lead and then, having broken into government and private computer systems, cripple or at least disable the military, financial, and service sectors of advanced economies. The growing dependence of our societies on information technology has created a new form of vulnerability, giving terrorists the chance to approach targets that would otherwise be utterly unassailable, such as national defense systems and air traffic control systems. The more technologically developed a country is, the more vulnerable it becomes to cyberattacks against its infrastructure.

Concern about the potential danger posed by cyberterrorism is thus well founded. That does not mean, however, that all the fears that have been voiced in the media, in Congress, and in other public forums are rational and reasonable. Some fears are simply unjustified, while others are highly exaggerated. In addition, the distinction between the potential and the actual damage inflicted by cyberterrorists has too often been ignored, and the relatively benign activities of most hackers have been conflated with the specter of pure cyberterrorism.

This report examines the reality of the cyberterrorism threat, present and future. It begins by outlining why cyberterrorism angst has gripped so many people, defines what qualifies as "cyberterrorism" and what does not, and charts cyberterrorism's appeal for terrorists. The report then looks at the evidence both for and against Western society's vulnerability to cyberattacks, drawing on a variety of recent studies and publications to illustrate the kinds of fears that have been expressed and to assess whether we need to be so concerned. The conclusion looks to the future and argues that we must remain alert to real dangers while not becoming victims of overblown fears.

Cyberterrorism Angst

The roots of the notion of cyberterrorism can be traced back to the early 1990s, when the rapid growth in Internet use and the debate on the emerging "information society" sparked several studies on the potential risks faced by the highly networked, high-tech-dependent United States. As early as 1990, the National Academy of Sciences began a report on computer security with the words, "We are at risk. Increasingly, America depends on computers. … Tomorrow's terrorist may be able to do more damage with a keyboard than with a bomb." At the same time, the prototypical term "electronic Pearl Harbor" was coined, linking the threat of a computer attack to an American historical trauma.

Psychological, political, and economic forces have combined to promote the fear of cyberterrorism. From a psychological perspective, two of the greatest fears of modern time are combined in the term "cyberterrorism." The fear of random, violent victimization blends well with the distrust and outright fear of computer technology. An unknown threat is perceived as more threatening than a known threat. Although cyberterrorism does not entail a direct threat of violence, its psychological impact on anxious societies can be as powerful as the effect of terrorist bombs. Moreover, the most destructive forces working against an understanding of the actual threat of cyberterrorism are a fear of the unknown and a lack of information or, worse, too much misinformation.

After 9/11, the security and terrorism discourse soon featured cyberterrorism prominently. This was understandable, given that more nightmarish attacks were expected and that cyberterrorism seemed to offer al Qaeda opportunities to inflict enormous damage. But there was also a political dimension to the new focus on cyberterrorism. Debates about national security, including the security of cyberspace, always attract political actors with agendas that extend beyond the specific issue at hand—and the debate over cyberterrorism was no exception to this pattern. For instance, Yonah Alexander, a terrorism researcher at the Potomac Institute—a think tank with close links to the Pentagon—announced in December 2001 the existence of an "Iraq Net." This network supposedly consisted of more than one hundred websites set up across the world by Iraq since the mid-nineties to launch denial-of-service (DoS) attacks against US companies (such attacks render computer systems inaccessible, unusable, or inoperable). "Saddam Hussein would not hesitate to use the cyber tool he has. . . . It is not a question of if but when. The entire United States is the front line," Alexander claimed. (See Ralf Bendrath's article "The American Cyber-Angst and the Real World," published in 2003 in *Bombs and*

Bandwidth, edited by Robert Latham.) Whatever the intentions of its author, such a statement was clearly likely to support arguments then being made for an aggressive US policy toward Iraq. No evidence of an Iraq Net has yet come to light.

Combating cyberterrorism has become not only a highly politicized issue but also an economically rewarding one. An entire industry has emerged to grapple with the threat of cyberterrorism: think tanks have launched elaborate projects and issued alarming whitepapers on the subject, experts have testified to cyberterrorism's dangers before Congress, and private companies have hastily deployed security consultants and software designed to protect public and private targets. Following the 9/11 attacks, the federal government requested $4.5 billion for infrastructure security, and the FBI now boasts more than one thousand "cyber investigators."

Before September 11, 2001, George W. Bush, then a presidential candidate, warned that "American forces are overused and underfunded precisely when they are confronted by a host of new threats and challenges—the spread of weapons of mass destruction, the rise of cyberterrorism, the proliferation of missile technology." After the 9/11 attacks, President Bush created the Office of Cyberspace Security in the White House and appointed his former counterterrorism coordinator, Richard Clarke, to head it. The warnings came now from the president, the vice president, security advisors, and government officials: "Terrorists can sit at one computer connected to one network and can create worldwide havoc," cautioned Tom Ridge, director of the Department of Homeland Security, in a representative observation in April 2003. "[They] don't necessarily need a bomb or explosives to cripple a sector of the economy or shut down a power grid." These warnings certainly had a powerful impact on the media, on the public, and on the administration. For instance, a survey of 725 cities conducted in 2003 by the National League of Cities found that cyberterrorism ranked alongside biological and chemical weapons at the top of a list of city officials' fears.

The mass media have added their voice to the fearful chorus, running scary front-page headlines such as the following, which appeared in the *Washington Post* in June 2003: "Cyber-Attacks by Al Qaeda Feared, Terrorists at Threshold of Using Internet as Tool of Bloodshed, Experts Say." Cyberterrorism, the media have discovered, makes for eye-catching, dramatic copy. Screenwriters and novelists have likewise seen the dramatic potential, with movies such as the 1995 James Bond feature, *Goldeneye,* and 2002's *Code Hunter* and novels such as Tom Clancy and Steve R. Pieczenik's *Netforce* popularizing a wide range of cyberterrorist scenarios.

The net effect of all this attention has been to create a climate in which instances of hacking into government websites, online thefts of proprietary data from companies, and outbreaks of new computer viruses are all likely to be labeled by the media as suspected cases of "cyberterrorism." Indeed, the term has been improperly used and overused to such an extent that, if we are to have any hope of reaching a clear understanding of the danger posed by cyberterrorism, we must begin by defining it with some precision.

[...]

Is the Cyberterror Threat Exaggerated?

Amid all the dire warnings and alarming statistics that the subject of cyberterrorism generates, it is important to remember one simple statistic: so far, there has been no recorded instance of a terrorist cyberattack on US public facilities, transportation systems, nuclear power plants, power grids, or other key components of the national infrastructure. Cyberattacks are common, but they have not been conducted by terrorists and they have not sought to inflict the kind of damage that would qualify them as cyberterrorism.

Technological expertise and use of the Internet do not constitute evidence of planning for a cyberattack. Joshua Green ("The Myth of Cyberterrorism," *Washington Monthly,* November 2002) makes this point after reviewing the data retrieved from terrorists in Afghanistan:

When US troops recovered al Qaeda laptops in Afghanistan, officials were surprised to find its members more technologically adept than previously believed. They discovered structural and engineering software, electronic models of a dam, and information on computerized water systems, nuclear power plants, and US and European stadiums. But nothing suggested they were planning cyberattacks, only that they were using the Internet to communicate and coordinate physical attacks.

Neither al Qaeda nor any other terrorist organization appears to have tried to stage a serious cyberattack. For now, insiders or individual hackers are responsible for most attacks and intrusions and the hackers' motives are not political. According to a report issued in 2002 by IBM Global Security Analysis Lab, 90 percent of hackers are amateurs with limited technical proficiency, 9 percent are more skilled at gaining unauthorized access but do not damage the files they read, and only 1 percent are highly skilled and intent on copying files or damaging programs and systems. Most hackers, it should be noted, try to expose security flaws in computer software, mainly in the operating systems produced by Microsoft. Their efforts in this direction have sometimes embarrassed corporations but have also been responsible for alerting the public and security professionals to serious security flaws. Moreover, although there are hackers with the ability to damage systems, disrupt e-commerce, and force websites offline, the vast majority of hackers do not have the necessary skills and knowledge. The ones who do, generally do not seek to wreak havoc. Douglas Thomas, a professor at the University of Southern California, spent seven years studying computer hackers in an effort to understand better who they are and what motivates them. Thomas interviewed hundreds of hackers and explored their "literature." In testimony on July 24, 2002, before the House Subcommittee on Government Efficiency, Financial Management and Intergovernmental Relations, Thomas argued that "with the vast majority of hackers, I would say 99 percent of them, the risk [of cyberterrorism] is negligible for the simple reason that those hackers do not have the skill or ability to organize or execute an attack that would be anything more than a minor inconvenience." His judgment was echoed in *Assessing the Risks of Cyberterrorism, Cyber War, and Other Cyber Threats*, a 2002 report for the Center for Strategic and International Studies, written by Jim Lewis, a sixteen-year veteran of the State and Commerce Departments. "The idea that hackers are going to bring the nation to its knees is too far-fetched a scenario to be taken seriously," Lewis argued. "Nations are more robust than the early analysts of cyberterrorism and cyberwarfare give them credit for. Infrastructure systems [are] more flexible and responsive in restoring service than the early analysts realized, in part because they have to deal with failure on a routine basis."

Many computer security experts do not believe that it is possible to use the Internet to inflict death on a large scale. Some pointed out that the resilience of computer systems to attack is the result of significant investments of time, money, and expertise. As Green describes, nuclear weapons systems are protected by "air-gapping": they are not connected to the Internet or to any open computer network and thus they cannot be accessed by intruders, terrorists, or hackers. Thus, for example, the Defense Department protects sensitive systems by isolating them from the Internet and even from the Pentagon's own internal network. The CIA's classified computers are also air-gapped, as is the FBI's entire computer system.

The 9/11 events and the subsequent growing awareness of cyberterror highlighted other potential targets for such attacks. In 2002, Senator Charles Schumer (D-N.Y.) described "the absolute havoc and devastation that would result if cyberterrorists suddenly shut down our air traffic control system, with thousands of planes in mid-flight." However, argues Green, "cybersecurity experts give some of their highest marks to the Federal Aviation Authority, which reasonably separates its administrative and air traffic control systems and strictly air-gaps the latter."

Other sources of concern include subway systems, gas lines, oil pipelines, power grids, communication systems, water dams, and public services that might be attacked to inflict mass destruction. Most of these are managed and controlled by computer systems and are in the private sector—and thus they are more vulnerable than military or government systems. To illustrate the threat of such attack, a story in the *Washington Post* in June 2003 on al Qaeda cyberterrorism related an anecdote about a teenage hacker who allegedly broke into the SCADA system at Arizona's Theodore Roosevelt Dam in 1998 and, according to the article, could have unleashed millions of gallons of water, imperiling neighboring communities. However, a probe by the computer-technology news site CNet.com revealed the story to be exaggerated and concluded that the hacker could not have endangered lives or property.

To assess the potential threat of cyberterrorism, experts such as Denning suggest that two questions be asked: Are there targets that are vulnerable to cyberattacks? And are there actors with the capability and motivation to carry out such attacks? The answer to the first question is yes: critical infrastructure systems are complex and therefore bound to contain weaknesses that might be exploited, and even systems that seem "hardened" to outside manipulation might be accessed by insiders, acting alone or in concert with terrorists, to cause considerable harm. But what of the second question?

According to Green, "few besides a company's own employees possess the specific technical know-how required to run a specialized SCADA system." There is, of course, the possibility of terrorists recruiting employees or ex-employees of targeted companies or systems. In April 2002, an Australian man attempted to use the Internet to release a million gallons of raw sewage along Queensland's Sunshine Coast. The police discovered that he had worked for the company that designed the sewage treatment plant's control software. It is possible, of course, that such disgruntled employees might be recruited by terrorist groups, but even if the terrorists did enlist inside help, the degree of damage they could cause would still be limited. As Green argues, the employees of companies that handle power grids, oil and gas utilities, and communications are well rehearsed in dealing with the fallout from hurricanes, floods, tornadoes, and other natural disasters. They are also equally adept at containing and remedying problems that stem from human action.

Denning draws our attention to a report, "Cyberterror: Prospects and Implications," published in August 1999 by the Center for the Study of Terrorism and Irregular Warfare at the Naval Postgraduate School (NPS) in Monterey, California. The report, explains Denning, shows that terrorists generally lack the wherewithal and human capital needed to mount attacks that involve more than annoying but relatively harmless hacks. The study examined five types of terrorist groups: religious, New Age, ethnonationalist separatist, revolutionary, and far-right extremist. Of these, only the religious groups were adjudged likely to seek the capacity to inflict massive damage. Hacker groups, the study determined, are psychologically and organizationally ill suited to cyberterrorism, and any massive disruption of the information infrastructure would run counter to their self-interest.

A year later, in October 2000, the NPS group issued a second report, this one examining the decision-making process by which substate groups engaged in armed resistance develop new operational methods, including cyberterrorism. This report also shows that while sub-state groups may find cyberterror attractive as a nonlethal weapon, terrorists have not yet integrated information technology into their strategy and tactics and that significant barriers between hackers and terrorists may prevent their integration into one group.

Another illustration of the limited likelihood of terrorists launching a highly damaging cyberattack comes from a simulation sponsored by the US Naval War College. The college contracted with a research group to simulate a massive cyberattack on the nation's information infrastructure. Government hackers and security analysts met in July 2002 in Newport, R.I., and conducted a joint war game dubbed "Digital Pearl Harbor." The results were far from devastating: the hackers failed to crash the Internet, although they did cause sporadic damage. According to a CNet.com report on the exercise published in August 2002, officials concluded that terrorists hoping to stage such an attack "would require a syndicate with significant resources, including $200 million, country-level intelligence and five years of preparation time."

[…]

Cyberattacks Do Not Cause Enough Damage to Count as Acts of Terrorism or War

Tate Watkins

Tate Watkins is a research fellow and managing editor at the Property and Environment Management Research Center. His writing has appeared in the Wall Street Journal, *the* Washington Post, Reason, *the* Atlantic, *and the* Hill.

Despite what your congressman may tell you, cyber war might never happen, says a researcher in the Department of War Studies at King's College London.

Thomas Rid, also a fellow at Johns Hopkins' School for Advanced International Studies, writes that "Cyber War Will Not Take Place," an assessment that contrasts with those of many elected US officials. Rid claims that no online attack to date constitutes cyber war and that it's "highly unlikely that cyber war will occur in the future."

For an online attack to constitute war, he writes, it would have to be "a potentially lethal, instrumental, and political act of force conducted through malicious code." Despite a lack of an on-the-record online attack that fulfills these criteria, and little evidence that one ever will, members of Congress have relentlessly touted a message of cyber doom in recent years.

"We are at war, we are being attacked, and we are being hacked," said Sen. Barbara Mikulski (D-Md.), when US Cyber Command headquarters were established in Maryland in 2010. Sens. Jay Rockefeller (D-W. Va.) and Olympia Snowe (R-Maine) published an op-ed in the *Wall Street Journal* last year titled, "Now Is the Time to Prepare for Cyberwar." Rockefeller and Snowe sponsored one of the numerous cybersecurity bills that have been proposed in the past two years.

"Cyber War: Still Not a Thing," by Tate Watkins, *Reason*, October 21, 2011. Reprinted by permission.

At a Senate hearing in 2010, Sen. Carl Levin (D-Mich.) said, "Cyber weapons and cyber attacks potentially can be devastating, approaching weapons of mass destruction in their effects." At a House hearing, Rep. Yvette Clarke (D-N.Y.) also implied that cyber threats are as dangerous as kinetic warfare, saying, "There is no more significant threat to our national and economic security than that which we face in cyberspace."

But, Rid writes, even previous politically motivated cyber attacks are "merely sophisticated versions of three activities that are as old as warfare itself: subversion, espionage, and sabotage."

His sentiments echo ones that Jerry Brito and I expressed in "The Cybersecurity-Industrial Complex: The feds erect a bureaucracy to combat a questionable threat," from the August/ September 2011 issue of *Reason*. Brito and I noted that warnings from members of Congress and government officials about online threats almost unfailingly include rhetoric about war, doom, or catastrophe. But the evidence they offer almost unfailingly relates to things like espionage, crime, vandalism, or flooding websites with traffic via distributed denial of service (DDoS) attacks.

We pointed out, as Rid does, that oft-cited examples of cyber war—like DDoS attacks on Estonian government and bank websites in 2007 and similar attacks against the nation of Georgia in 2008— do not constitute war. Rid notes that the attacks against Estonia fail to pass the criteria that render an attack "war": namely, that it's potentially lethal, instrumental, and political:

> Unlike a naval blockade, the mere "blockade" of websites is not violent, not even potentially; unlike a naval blockade, the DDoS attack was not instrumentally tied to a tactical objective, but an act of undirected protest; and unlike ships blocking the way, the pings remained anonymous, without political backing.

One government official who has laudably countered the cyber war rhetoric is White House cybersecurity coordinator Howard Schmidt. "There is no cyberwar," Schmidt told Wired.com in 2010. "I think that is a terrible metaphor and I think that is a terrible concept."

CHAPTER 3

Should Governments Be Responsible for Preventing Cyberterrorism?

Overview: The UN and Various Countries Have Protocols and Positions on Cyberterrorism

Nick Myers

Nick Myers received his bachelor's degree in political science and international affairs at Old Dominion University, where he was involved in Model UN.

Technology has revolutionized the interconnectedness of the globe. The flagship of that globalization is the Internet. However, like all other interconnecting technologies before it, the Internet can become a weapon in the eyes of states, criminals, and terrorists alike. Known as either cyber war or cyber conflict, these attempts to disrupt information technology systems have provoked an increasingly desperate debate on how to respond.

As UN Member States struggle to protect their networks and linked infrastructure from disruption, security against foreign-based attacks has become vital. Member States are concerned about the potential to affect individuals, corporations, states, and regional systems. The anonymity of attacks is a major part of the problem; attackers can swiftly disable individuals, government agencies and private firms, without revealing who carried out the attack in the first place.

Given the transnational nature of many of these attacks, international organizations like the UN have been increasingly pressured to address the rise of cyber-attacks and the security measures against them in the hope of eliciting new international regulations regarding cyber security. Yet, the UN is not without problems of its own in addressing the issues surrounding cyber security and cyber terrorism.

Broadly, the UN is faced with a major roadblock related to cyber. Member States have varied positions on whether the UN should have oversight over what a nation does in cyberspace. Some Member States insist current international laws can sufficiently deal with cyber threats. Other Member States fear expanding international law will be used to narrow their national power, or might undermine their freedom of action.

Currently, cyberspace is viewed as an extension of international law, meaning cyber-attacks are viewed as legally the same as physical attacks rather than as separate issue without its own norms. There is some interest within the General Assembly and the Security Council to address cyber threats by creating new norms for cyber response and use. But the disconnect between the international dangers and national capabilities in cyberspace weakens the potential for forceful UN action, even when it is needed most.

Many Member States want the entire UN community to take an active role responding to the threats posed by cyber-attacks. They say that more effort needs to be put into this issue within the General Assembly especially, since that is where global moral principles are agreed. The current ambiguity surrounding cyber-attacks leaves long standing questions about the definition and meaning of an attack and its consequences in doubt. The ambiguity undoubtedly helps attackers and those who would use the Internet for malicious purposes.

Growing demands for new rules and approaches to cyberspace have been heard from several Member States. This shift led to several resolutions over the past few years. But other Member States worry that international action could be a veil for efforts to restrict their freedom of action, or advance the particular interests of specific countries. Where growing demands for action will lead is hard to judge.

In an ever-integrating global economy, the prospect of cyber threats looms over everyone. The U.N. remains the most prominent forum for addressing global issues. Important steps have been taken to address these threats, including in the General Assembly, Security Council, and several UN technical organizations. These have established important principles to guide international action. But calls for more aggressive action have gone unmet. If Member States wish for a true universal approach to solving the issues of cyberspace, more work needs to be done.

[...]

The emerging issue of cyber security has made it a relevant issue to all UN organizations, either because those bodies utilize the Internet or because they are responsible for ensuring access and protecting state interests. While the UN has condemned all types of cybercrime and attempted to increase access to defensive technologies, it has also failed to sufficiently address the issue. Rival interests and priorities of Member States make it difficult for the UN to agree on basic principles. The lack of focused attention on cyber security, cyber terrorism, and cyber-attacks has slowed forceful action against cyber terrorism and cybercrime. Part of this is simply because cyberspace is such a large and complicated subject, hard to pack into even a few organizations or resolutions.

A more fundamental weakness comes from the tendency of the international community to view cyber threats as a new branch of existing issues.

For example, the UN couples human trafficking and cyber trafficking as a single trans-national crime issue, treating cybercrime as an extension of other kinds of crime under international law. While appropriate for an organization to attempt to work against broad-reaching criminal organizations, this coupling of other issues to cyber inhibits the development of new norms, resolutions, and agreements tailored to addressing cyber-specific issues on the broad spectrum of cyber security concerns. Thus, no new, global cyber laws have been created to treat these as unique issues.

Critics say this leads to a false feeling of adequacy within the organization, a comfort in the familiar capabilities of sub-organizations to address issues like crime or terrorism. Yet, without a unique cyber-specific sub-organization it becomes difficult for the UN to respond to the changing situation surrounding cyber as a whole, thus serving to highlight a disconnect between wanting to act on cyber as a specific Member State and the organization as a whole feeling comfortable with the inadequate status quo despite the increasing frequency of prominent cyber-attacks.

Finally, the existing UN system on cyber threats is paralyzed to address cyber issues once they arise. Frequently, the General Assembly or Security Council will not mention cyber, with it coming up less than 5 times in the last 3 years.[10] Given the volume of cyber-attacks occurring each year coupled with the dynamic nature of cyber, this is remarkably low. If the subject is brought up, there is usually disagreement about how a global effort to combat cyber threats would work, with states such as Russia wanting more universal participation in creating mandates on cyberspace involving all members through an inclusive Open-Ended Working Group (OEWG), while the US and UK want top ranking members to report on and create mandates for the rest of the world via a Group of Governmental Experts (GGE).[11] There is no denying that the UN and its members want to create a more stream-lined cyber strategy, but endless in-body debates means any universal acceptance of new laws and cyber security remains unlikely if there is not a vast uptick in discussion and relevance of cyber within the UN as there is disagreement regarding how the organization should respond to future developments.

Despite these shortcomings, there remain several entities working on cyber security and assisting the UN. The Geneva-based International Telecommunications Union (ITU), an independent international organization affiliated with the United Nations, has emerged as the center for international coordination on these issues. By setting standards for all telecommunications, it provides essential benchmarks for governments, establishing what is universally accepted as permissible and where limits are for governments. UN General Assembly and ECOSOC relations usually mandate the ITU as the center for further consideration and action. The ITU has set up a global cyber security index (GCI) in an effort to bring more attention to cyber threats worldwide in coordination with the UN.[12] This is meant to keep an up active list of both cyber-attacks and useful strategies to defend against attacks so Member States can better deal with cyber security issues. The ITU also assists in designing cyber security plans and infrastructure for member states.

Other, smaller bodies within working to combat cyber terrorism include the UNOCT's Cybersecurity Programme, which focuses on enhancing state capacity and private organizations in preventing cyber-attacks, and the Office on Drugs and Crime's (UNODC) Global Programme on Cybercrime, which focuses on capacity building and technical assistance of cyber networks and defensive systems. These bodies offer the main source of energy and effort in combatting cyber-attacks and improving security for Member States, but each of these organizations is limited due to lacking the support of a coordinating mechanism to assist each disparate UN organization in addressing cyber security developments together. Thus, the UN is left with several organizations going in different directions rather than a unified approach capable of constructing international norms, regulations, or mandates.

Taken as a whole, this reveals a UN framework that is hardly adequate for a weapon system and problem which is rapidly transforming, becoming more prevalent, and holds the potential to significantly disrupt global relations. Inaction can only take the UN so far, and the cobbled together nature of current UN programs indicates the issue is setting the pace for the organization rather than the organization being proactive in developing a regime for the future.

Landmark UN Resolutions

Over the past several years there have been attempts to turn the UN to address cyber security and cyber issues uniquely through resolutions within the Security Council and the General Assembly. Unfortunately, very few of these resolutions broke enough ground to be truly transformative for UN policy, but they remain influential in being the most significant efforts within the most significant international bodies to do something regarding cyber issues.

Security Council resolution 2341 (passed in 2017), established a process, continuing to this day, to establish "best practices" to protect critical infrastructure from cyber-attacks in coordination with Interpol, UN Counter-Terrorism Centre, and the Counter-Terrorism Committee Executive Directorate.[13] This helps states stay informed about potential cyber risks they need to counter.

General Assembly resolution 74/173 (2019) focused primarily on development of Member States capacity building to respond to cybercrime brought in components of cooperative objectives.[14]

General Assembly resolution 74/28 (2019) presented standards for responsible state behavior in cyberspace for international security purposes.[15] Of greatest importance was establishing international norms, regulations, laws, and non-binding resolutions to cyber technology environments.

General Assembly resolution 73/266 (2018) focused on the development and codification of international principles for cyberspace, with a particular focus on the impacts of it financially.[16]

General Assembly resolution 73/187 (2018) on countering criminal activity, seeks more international cooperation to stop criminal organizations utilizing communications platforms to commit crimes.[17] Importantly it called for improving the technical infrastructure of developing states to address this concern through assistance through the UN.

These resolutions illustrate an attempt to develop a response to challenges related to cyber developments, but fall short of providing a landmark policy trajectory for the UN. Instead, they establish the importance of the issue, the role of the UN on the subject, and the potential dangers for states ignoring the problem.

Country and Bloc Positions

Issues like cyber security attract a host of differing opinions, beliefs, and philosophies concerning the role of international governance, institutions, and the role of the state within cyber space. Broadly, states divide into two camps where the first believes cyberspace should be the purview of states and the second believing there is a critical role for international governance in cyberspace. Interestingly, several states only became concerned over the developments related to cyber because they have experienced significant cyber-attacks recently including Australia,[18] India,[19] and Indonesia. Other critical players on the issue include:

China

Famous for the "Great Firewall" that blocks mostly European and UN tech firms from its internet, China has stressed its sovereign control over all other goals. Second, it seeks to expend influence, through its own firms, and through control over UN agencies. China has readily adopted, utilized, and developed cyber capabilities at an astounding rate.[20] Viewing cyber space as a new realm for interacting within the international community, China specifically focuses on its own domestic information security to prevent dissent. It favors international cooperation in response to threats while retaining its own state autonomy.

Democratic Republic of Korea (North Korea)

Although it is not a major force in the UN North Korea could be a target of future UN resolutions. North Korea represents an interesting major player when it comes to cyber security concerns.[21] Favoring asymmetric cyberattacks geared towards disrupting target operations and provocations to justify domestic considerations, North Korea was considered responsible for the Sony Hack in 2014.[22] Additionally domestic censorship and propaganda are heavily utilized. North Korea is widely believed to use cyber activity to augment state income, overcoming UN sanctions to a degree.

European Union

The EU and its 27 Member States have been ardent supporters of user information security. They have repeatedly challenged the dominance of American tech firms, and increasingly question those from China, too.[23] In terms of addressing cyber-attacks and terrorism, the EU has established several regional organizations to address the issue. In a move that anticipates its priorities for the UN, it established the EU Cybersecurity Act in February 2020.[24] The EU is highly sensitive to Internet security, and especially insistent that the privacy and rights of private users be protected from spying by governments.

Iran

Iran has been both a victim and originator of cyber conflict. In 2009 is was attacked by Israel and the US through their Olympic Games (Stuxnet) campaign to temporarily disable part of its nuclear infrastructure. Iran also has been a willing participant in the development of cyber capabilities to address cyber defense and attacks.[25] The Iranian history of significant cyber-attacks is quite large, with a heavy reliance on attacking critical systems for opposing states.[26] Most recently following the American assassination of General Qassem Soleimani, the threat of Iranian cyber-attacks increased.[27] In the UN, Iran favors a state-centered approach to cyber security issues like cyber attack.

Non-Aligned Movement

For the 120 Member States of UN's largest voting bloc, development aspects outrank other concerns. NAM Member States may be willing to join resolutions to tighten international standards or support action against specific countries, even fellow NAM members like DPR Korea or Iran. In exchange they will insist on generous development assistance, such as financial support for their national broadband networks and cyber law enforcement capabilities. The NAM focuses on the threat that fast-changing information and technologies could be used for purposes that are contradictory with maintaining international law and stability.[28] Many in the NAM have proposed that a legal framework be developed within the UN to combat these rising issues.

Russia

Although fiercely denied by its leaders and spokesmen, Russia is widely suspected of major Internet and social media attacks against infrastructure (such as electricity generation), news media and electoral systems in countries like Ukraine, the UK and US.[29] Yet, Russia has also been an ardent supporter of UN actions to curtail cybercrime. A significant resolution was passed through the General Assembly, written by Russia.[30] In this sense, Russia has become increasingly skilled at navigating the processes of the UN to further their approach to cyber governance which has been criticized as "digital authoritarianism." They also helped create the OEWG, being the main state to propose new rules and a more universal recognition of cyber. Russia has recently released a statement on the issue of cyber security in lieu of the Covid-19 pandemic.

The United States

American cyber security policy focuses on combatting cyber-attacks by securing America's domestic networks and critical infrastructures, along with expanding American influence and norms internationally.[31] The US believes that international cyber stability and conflict prevention are best advanced by current international law. Recently, the US has been increasingly aggressive towards cyber threats, increasingly striking suspected threats preemptively. Part of this includes being more open in declaring the suspected culprits of cyberattacks. Cyber has become a massive part of American defense and foreign policy, with proposals in 2019 made by the Cyberspace Solarium Commission to work more closely with the private sector in sharing information with agencies like the NSA and Cybersecurity and Infrastructure Security Agency (CISA).

Proposals for Action

The UN response to cyber space is still in its infancy, thus the only precedence lies in similar issues which could be capable in informing or framing resolutions. The pre-existing resolutions offer a framework to proceed in addressing issues related to cyber security, but be aware of what kind of action the UN has undertaken, whether it be setting up the Group of Governmental Experts to make reports on the use of cyber space, or sub-organizations like UNODC, UNOCT, and the ITU. These all focus on improving knowledge and security of Member States and businesses against cyber terrorism and crime. Some potential proposals to consider include:

- Require Internet service providers—the companies that make the Internet work—to monitor and enforce restrictions on use of the Internet to harm the infrastructure or interests of UN Member States. This could be especially popular in Member States that already restrict private Internet activity. It will be opposed by Member States were personal freedom and privacy are more important.
- Establish an independent UN agency to monitor Internet activity and report to Member States on Internet use and attacks by their citizens or foreign sources. This also could be especially popular in Member States that already restrict private Internet activity. It will be opposed by Member States were personal freedom and privacy are more important. Financing and staffing for the new agencies would have to be established.
- Propose a global definition of cyber terrorism, cyber-attacks, cyber security as part of an effort to establish a foundation for new international laws, rules, and norms.
- Provide technical assistance to states to increase their security capabilities against potential cyber-attacks. Financing and

paying for technical assistance could be a problem, but countries interested in expanding their global influence might be willing to subsidize such a resolution, if it favors their firms.

- Sponsor the development of a UN framework organization to coordinate all cyber security responses and considerations.
- Encourage Member States to prepare their own defenses. Such a limited proposal might be most popular with Member States determined to protect their national sovereignty and avoid new obligations.
- Establish rules for sanctioning states responsible for carrying out, funding, or assisting in cyber-attacks against other states, international organizations, or corporations.
- Finance the development of offensive cyber capabilities in order to establish deterrent measures to prevent cyber-attacks.
- Provide the means for the revival of the typewriter construction industry and other intranet systems. After all, states cannot hack what is not connected to the internet.

Endnotes

10. *General Assembly Resolutions.* New York: United Nations, 2020, www.un.org /en/sections/documents/general-assembly-resolutions/

11. *Group of Governmental Experts.* New York: United Nations Office for Disarmament Affairs, 2019, www.un.org/disarmament/group-of -governmental-experts/

12. *United Nations Launches Global Cybersecurity Index.* Geneva: International Telecommunication Union, n.d., https://www.itu.int/en/ITU- D /Cybersecurity/Pages/United-Nations-Launches- Global-Cybersecurity -Index.aspx

13. *The protection of critical infrastructure against terrorist attacks: Compendium of good practices.* Vienna: United Nations Counter-Terrorism Centre, 2018, https://www.un.org/sc/ctc/wp- content/uploads/2018/06/Compendium-CIP -final- version- 120618_new_fonts_18_june_2018_optimized.pdf

14. *Promoting technical assistance and capacity-building to strengthen national measures and international cooperation to combat cybercrime, including information-sharing,* resolution 74/173. New York: United Nations, 2019, https://undocs.org/en/A/RES/74/173

15. *Advancing responsible State behaviour in cyberspace in the context of international security*, resolution 74/28. New York: United Nations, 2019, https://undocs.org/en/A/RES/74/28

16. *Advancing responsible State behaviour in cyberspace in the context of international security*, resolution 73/266. New York: United Nations, 2018, https://undocs.org/en/A/RES/73/266

17. *Countering the use of information and communications technologies for criminal purposes*, resolution 73/187. New York: United Nations, 2018, https://undocs.org/en/A/RES/73/187

18. Hafizah Osman, "Cyber security a top priority in Australia: Deloitte," *Tech Advisor*, 1 November 2012, https://www.techadvisor.co.uk/feature/security/cyber-security-top-priority-in-australia-deloitte-3408391/

19. Ashish Rajadhyaksha, *In the Wake of Aadhaar: The Digital Ecosystem of Governance in India*. Bangalore, 2013, https://egov.eletsonline.com/2012/11/government-to-invest-200-mn-in-4-yrs-on-cyber-security-infrastructure/; https://www.dnaindia.com/india/report-india-uk-to-conduct-talks-bi-annually-on-cyber-security-1762061

20. Lyu Jinghua, "What Are China's Cyber Capabilities and Intentions?" *Carnegie Endowment for International Peace*, 1 April 2019, https://carnegieendowment.org/2019/04/01/what-are-china-s-cyber-capabilities-and-intentions-pub-78734

21. www.csis-website-prod.s3.amazonaws.com/s3fs-public/legacy_files/files/publication/151216_Cha_No rthKoreasCyberOperations_Web.pdf

22. Andrea Peterson, "The Sony Pictures hack, explained," *Washington Post*, 18 December 2014, https://www.washingtonpost.com/news/the-switch/wp/2014/12/18/the-sony-pictures-hack-explained/

23. *Cybersecurity in Europe: stronger rules and better protection*. Brussels: European Council and the Council of the EU, 31 July 2020, https://www.consilium.europa.eu/en/policies/cyberse curity/

24. *The EU Cybersecurity Act*. Brussels; European Commission, 28 February 2020, https://ec.europa.eu/digital-single-market/en/eu-cybersecurity-act

25. James Andrew Lewis, "Iran and Cyber Power," *Center for Strategic and International Studies*, 25 June 2019, https://www.csis.org/analysis/iran-and-cyber-power

26. *Significant Cyber Incidents*, op.cit., https://www.csis.org/programs/technology-policy-program/significant-cyber-incidents

27. *National Terrorism Advisory System Bulletin*, Washington, D.C.: US Department of Homeland Security, 4 January 2020, https://www.dhs.gov/ntas/advisory/national-terrorism-advisory-system-bulletin-january-4-2020

28. "Calling for Norms to Stymie Cyberattacks, First Committee Speakers Say States Must Work Together in Preventing Information Arms Race," New York: UN General Assembly, 24 October 2016, www.un.org/press/en/2016/gadis3560.doc.htm

29. Tim Maurer and Garrett Hinck, "Russia's Cyber Strategy," Milan: Italian Institute for International Political Studies, 21 December 2018, www.ispionline .it/en/pubblicazione/russias-cyber-strategy-21835; www.russiaun.ru/en/news /arria_220520

30. https://www.washingtonpost.com/politics/2019/12/04 /un-passed-russia -backed-cybercrime-resolution-thats-not-good-news-internet-freedom/

31. President Donald J. Trump, *National Cyber Strategy of the United States of America, September 2018*. Washington, D.C.: The White House, 2018, www .whitehouse.gov/wp-content/uploads/2018/09/National-Cyber-Strategy .pdf; "Cyber-defence: America rethinks its strategy in the Wild West of cyberspace," *The Economist*, 28 May 2020, www.economist.com/united -states/2020/05/28/america-rethinks-its-strategy-in-the-wild-west-of -cyberspace

International Political Cooperation Is Essential to Fighting Cyberterrorism

Anna-Maria Talihärm

Anna-Maria Talihärm is a senior analyst of the Legal and Policy Branch at the NATO Cooperative Cyber Defence Centre of Excellence. She holds a degree in information technology law from Stockholm University. Her areas of research include European Union information society law, cyberterrorism, and cybercrime.

The ubiquitous use of information and communication technologies (ICT) serves both as an enabler of growth and innovation as well as the source of asymmetrical cyberthreats. Around the globe, about 2 million people are connected to the Internet, and the use of the Internet and ICT-enabled services is becoming more and more an indispensible part of our everyday lives. With the increasing dependence on ICT and the interlinked nature with critical infrastructure, we have become alarmingly vulnerable to possible disruption and exploitation by malicious cyberactivities.

Malicious cyberactivities have been affecting individuals, private entities, government institutions and non-governmental organizations for years. We have witnessed large-scale cyber-incidents such as in Estonia in 2007, with numerous sophisticated targeted attacks, hacktivism and countless instances of identity theft and malware. Due to the unpredictable nature of cyberthreats, an incident that may appear in the beginning as an act of hacktivism or financially motivated cybercrime may rapidly escalate into something much more serious and reach the threshold of national security, even cyberwar.

Despite the lack of consensus on exactly what constitutes cyberwarfare or cyberterrorism, governments need to ensure that their infrastructure is well protected against different types of cyberthreats and that their legal and policy frameworks would allow to effectively prevent, deter, defend and mitigate possible cyberattacks. Not being able to agree on common definitions of central terms such as "cyberattack" and "cyberwar" should not prevent states from expressing the urgency of preparing their nations for possible cyberincidents.

International Cooperation

The logic of international cooperation and collaboration lies on why, when, and how to collaborate, and generally takes place in order to follow one's interests or to manage common aversions.[1] In the context of cybersecurity, the need for international cooperation between states, international and regional organizations and other entities is emphasized by the borderless and increasingly sophisticated nature of cyberthreats. Principally, any actor, whether it is a country or a non-governmental organization, following its objectives in cybersecurity requires cooperation from a wide range of international partners. In fact, much of the international collaboration will occur outside specific national frameworks, emphasizing the Whole of System approach that stresses the need to take into account all relevant stakeholders.[2]

Thus, from a national perspective, advancements in cybersecurity depend to a large extent on the political will of different actors. Areas such as information and intelligence sharing and mutual assistance may become essential in responding to a cybercrisis, but the effectiveness of such cooperation depends greatly upon strategically aligned policy goals and bilateral and multilateral relations. In many domains, such as international criminal cooperation, there are several preconditions that need to be in place in the cooperating countries, such as substantive national law as well as procedural law and international agreements, before the dialogue on the possibility of any sort of international cooperation can grow into further discussions on the efficiency of such cooperation.

International Organizations Active in Cybersecurity

National policies, international agreements as well as other initiatives addressing cybersecurity that are being proposed and launched by different international, regional and national actors may vary considerably in their scope, aim and success, but they all underline the international dimension of cyberspace.

For example, the United Nations First Committee has been actively examining the Developments in the Field of Information and Telecommunications in the Context of International Security for years. The African Union has published the Draft African Union Convention on the Establishment of a Credible Legal Framework for Cyber Security in Africa. The European Union (EU) has recently published a Joint Communication on the Cyber Security Strategy of the European Union, which is the first attempt for a comprehensive EU policy document in this domain to reflect the common view on cybersecurity of all its 27 member states.

Even though in recent years the wider debate has intensified on the development of possible norms of behaviour or a set of confidence-building measures in the cybersecurity domain, it should not be forgotten that most of the pressing issues and challenges in areas related to cybersecurity have roots in the adoption and review of national legislation and the implementation of multilaterally agreed principles.

Principle Developments

The NATO Cooperative Cyber Defence Centre of Excellence (NATO CCD COE) is a North Atlantic Treaty Organization (NATO) accredited international military organization that focuses on a range of aspects related to cybersecurity, such as education, analyses, consultation, lessons learned, research and development. Even though the Centre does not belong to the direct command line of NATO, its mission is to enhance the capability, cooperation and information sharing among NATO, NATO nations and partners in cyberdefence.

Determined that international cooperation is key to the successful mitigation of cyberthreats worldwide, the Centre invests not only in broader collaboration with NATO and EU entities but, more specifically, focuses on improving practical cooperation within and among its sponsoring nations by hosting a real time network defence exercise known as Locked Shields. It also participates in many other similar simulations, thereby allowing the participants to put national coordination and cooperation frameworks to practise, and to learn and test the skills needed to fend off a real attack.

Regarding the legal and policy aspects of cybersecurity, NATO CCD COE has identified two main trends. Firstly, a growing number of countries are adopting national cybersecurity strategies and the majority of these documents confirm the role of cybersecurity as a national security priority. To further analyse such a development and the concept of national cybersecurity strategies, the Centre has conducted a comparative study called the National Cyber Security Framework Manual. The research asserts that a comprehensive cybersecurity strategy needs to take into account a number of national stakeholders with various responsibilities in ensuring national cybersecurity. The national stakeholders include critical infrastructure providers, law enforcement agencies, international organizations, computer emergency response teams and entities ensuring internal and external security. Importantly, instead of viewing cybersecurity as a combination of segregated areas or isolated stakeholders, the activities of different subdomains and areas of competence should be coordinated. Secondly, there are ongoing discussions about the applicability of international law to cyberactivities. Whereas it is widely accepted that cyberspace needs to be protected like air, sea and land, and is clearly defined by NATO Strategic Concept as a threat that can possibly reach a threshold setting threatening national and Euro-Atlantic prosperity, security and stability, there are only a few international agreements that would directly address behaviour in cyberspace.

Agreeing on a common stance even in matters regarding well-established norms of customary international law, such as the prohibition of the use of force codified in the United Nations Charter, Article 2(4), together with the two exceptions of self-defence and a resolution by the Security Council, in the context of their applicability to the cyberdomain remains a challenging task for the involved parties.

Therefore, amid the complex legal issues surrounding these debates, in 2009 NATO CCD COE invited an independent International Group of Experts to examine whether existing international law applies to issues regarding cybersecurity and, if so, to what extent. The result of this three-year project, the Tallinn Manual on the International Law Applicable to Cyber Warfare, focuses on the jus ad bellum, the international law governing the resort to force by states as an instrument of their national policy, and the jus in bello, the international law regulating the conduct of armed conflict. The experts taking part in the project concluded that, in principle, jus ad bellum and jus in bello do apply in the cyber context but this may be altered by state practice. This and other opinions expressed in the Tallinn Manual should not be considered as an official declaration of any state or organization, but rather as the interpretation of the group of individual international experts acting solely in their personal capacity. The Manual does not, however, address cyberactivities that occur below the threshold of a use of force, and for that purpose NATO CCD COE has launched a follow-on three-year project entitled Tallinn 2.0.

In order to prepare nations for possible cyberincidents and ensure a solid ground for international cooperation, both comprehensive national cybersecurity strategies and a common understanding on the applicability of the international law are required.

Even though it has been argued that multilateral treaties are the most practical vehicles for harmonizing national legal systems and aligning the interpretation of existing international law, discussions about moving towards such an agreement on a global level appear to be at a very early stage. Given the current normative ambiguity surrounding international law in the context of cybersecurity, international cooperation between different actors is deemed to be the cornerstone of effective responses to cyberthreats.

Notes

1. Choucri, Nazli. Cyberpolitics in International Relations (MIT Press, 2012), pp. 155-156.

2 . Klimburg, Alexander (ed.). National Cyber Security Framework Manual (NATO CCD COE, 2012).

Mandatory Cybersecurity Standards Would Protect Businesses and Infrastructure

Tom Gjelten

Tom Gjelten reports on religion, faith, and belief for NPR News. He started working for NPR in 1986 as one of its first foreign correspondents. He has also contributed to the New York Times, *the* Wall Street Journal, *the* Washington Post, *the* Atlantic, *and other publications.*

Consider what Hurricane Katrina did to New Orleans, and you get an idea of the consequences of a cyberattack on critical US infrastructure: No electricity. No water. No transportation. Terrorists or enemy adversaries with computer skills could conceivably take down a power grid, a nuclear station, a water treatment center or a chemical manufacturing plant.

The prospect of such a paralyzing strike has convinced US security officials and members of Congress that a new law may be needed to promote improved cyberdefenses at critical facilities around the country. Progress on that legislation, however, has been slowed by a debate over whether new cybersecurity measures should be mandated or merely encouraged.

The proposal that has received the most attention, sponsored by Sens. Joe Lieberman, I-Conn., Susan Collins, R-Maine, and others, would require owners and operators of critical infrastructure assets to notify the Department of Homeland Security of any and all cyber intrusions into their operating systems. Currently, such reporting is strictly voluntary, and security experts say only a fraction of the incidents come to the government's attention.

Heavy-Handed?

The Lieberman-Collins initiative would also establish baseline cybersecurity standards that all companies in an industrial sector would be required to meet. The legislation, however, has run into stiff opposition from private firms, the Chamber of Commerce and from members of Congress who view it as heavy-handed.

"Unelected bureaucrats at the [Department of Homeland Security] could promulgate prescriptive regulations on American businesses," charges Sen. John McCain, R-Ariz., the co-author of an alternative cybersecurity bill that favors voluntary information sharing between the government and private industry.

Advocates of mandatory cybersecurity standards, however, say the owners and operators of critical assets have consistently underestimated their vulnerability to cyberattacks and therefore are unlikely on their own to take the steps necessary to bolster their own defenses, particularly if they cost money.

Many operators, for example, do not realize their industrial controls may be accessible via the Internet.

Awareness of Weaknesses

Such was the conclusion of Sean McGurk, who visited hundreds of power stations, water-treatment facilities and other critical assets as director of the National Cybersecurity and Communications Integration Center at the Department of Homeland Security.

"In every case, we were told that the systems were completely isolated from the enterprise network or the Internet, that there were no direct connections," McGurk recalls. "And in no case has that ever been true. In hundreds of vulnerability assessments, we've always found connections between the equipment on the manufacturing floor and the outside world."

The operating equipment probably lacked online links when designed and installed, but modernization and automation in subsequent years have introduced network connections of which the operators may be unaware. Such connections offer a doorway through which cyberattackers can penetrate an industrial system.

DHS cybersecurity experts such as McGurk (who has since left the government) have so far been handicapped in addressing infrastructure vulnerabilities because nearly 90 percent of the installations are in private hands.

Awareness of those vulnerabilities varies widely among the owners and operators of infrastructure assets, and some are openly skeptical of the need for expensive new security measures.

"There's been an awful lot written about cybersecurity and the threat of it," said Robert Johnston, president and CEO of MEAG Power in Atlanta. "There are a lot of people who want to spend a huge amount of money on something that we have not necessarily identified."

Johnston made his comments last fall in an interview with *Energybiz*, a business journal.

"Show me an event where we've lost systems due to cyberterrorism," he said. "I'm not aware of one."

"A Window of Opportunity"

Security experts argue, however, that the example of the attacks of Sept. 11, 2001, shows that preparations for a terrorist attack must be made ahead of time.

"If terrorist groups were able to acquire these destructive cyber capabilities, I think we should fear greatly that they would use them," says William Lynn, until recently the deputy US secretary of defense. "The capabilities are not yet in the hands of the most malicious actors, so we have a window of opportunity to improve our defenses.

"We don't know exactly how long that window of opportunity is, but I think we should feel a strong need to improve our defenses before that happens."

The debate over whether to establish compulsory or voluntary cybersecurity standards has led to competing legislative proposals on Capitol Hill. Rep. James Langevin, D-R.I., for example, is pushing to increase the authority of the Federal Energy Regulatory Commission to monitor cybersecurity in the US power grid.

At present, FERC only has the power to approve or reject proposals initiated by power companies.

"I'd like to see that change," Langevin says, "so that when you have actionable intelligence that suggests a vulnerability exists and needs to be closed, FERC as the regulating entity has the authority to do that."

McCain and other Republican lawmakers have vigorously opposed such changes, saying industry is already overregulated and that new restrictions would hurt business.

"The regulations [under consideration] would stymie job creation, blur the definition of private property rights, and divert resources from actual cybersecurity to compliance with government mandates," McCain argued during a recent congressional hearing on proposed legislation.

Profits over Public Safety?

Langevin and others have countered that private owners and operators may need to be forced to improve their cybersecurity for the general good.

"I would assess that the owners and operators of critical infrastructure have employed a minimum level of security because employing more robust cybersecurity would cost money and affect the bottom line," Langevin says. "They're putting profits ahead of public safety, in my opinion."

The wrangling over cybersecurity, however, is not strictly partisan. Among the advocates of tough, compulsory measures are several former Bush administration officials, including Michael Chertoff, a former secretary of Homeland Security, and Michael McConnell, a former director of National Intelligence, as well as FBI Director Robert Mueller, who has served under both Presidents Obama and Bush.

McConnell is especially dismissive of the argument that the mandatory cybersecurity measures being proposed would be anti-business.

"You got the same argument with virtually everything from seat belts to safety devices in electrical equipment," he says. "If you're out competing, and the competition is tough, you don't want to add any cost to your process, so your natural response to any regulatory talk is, 'It's more burden, and it's not worth it, and it would put me at a competitive disadvantage.'"

Though McConnell calls himself "a free-market advocate," he argues that more government regulation is sometimes needed, including in the cyber domain.

"This threat is so intrusive, it's so serious," he says. "If we don't address it, it's going to have a severe impact. I think we have no choice but to address it, and some of that process will be regulatory."

Still, some compromise will be necessary if new cybersecurity legislation is to be approved, and any final bill will undoubtedly promote some kind of government-industry partnership.

McGurk, who is now in private business helping firms address their cybersecurity problems, says such cooperative efforts are essential.

"With very limited exceptions, the skills necessary to secure water companies and power companies and chemical companies and nuclear facilities are nowhere available in the federal government," he says. "They reside in the private sector, with the asset owners and operators."

Active Defense Against Cyberattacks by Private Corporations and Organizations Could Do More Harm Than Good

Scott Shackelford

Scott Shackelford is an associate professor of business law and ethics at Indiana University, where he is also executive director of the Ostrom Workshop and the cybersecurity program chair. He teaches cybersecurity law and policy, sustainability, and international business law.

The deluge of cyberattacks sweeping across the world has governments and companies thinking about new ways to protect their digital systems, and the corporate and state secrets stored within. For a long time, cybersecurity experts have erected firewalls to keep out unwanted traffic and set up decoy targets on their networks to distract hackers who do get in. They have also scoured the internet for hints about what cybercriminals might be up to next to better protect themselves and their clients.

Now, though, many leaders and officials are starting to think about stepping up their defensive activities, by taking more active measures. An extreme option within this field of active defense is sometimes called "hacking back" into an adversary's systems to get clues about what they're doing, shut down the attack or even delete data or otherwise damage an attacker's computers.

I have been researching the benefits and drawbacks of various active defense options with Danuvasin Charoen of the Thai National Institute of Development Administration and Kalea Miao, an undergraduate Cox scholar at the Indiana University Kelley School of Business. We have found a surprising number and variety of firms—and countries—exploring various ways to be more proactive in their cybersecurity practices, often with little fanfare.

Getting Active

On the surface, it might seem like the proverb is right: "The best defense is a good offense." The damage from cyberattacks can be enormous: In May 2017, a single incident, the WannaCry cyberattack, affected hundreds of thousands of systems around the world and caused more than US$4 billion in lost productivity and data recovery costs. One month later, another attack, called NotPetya, cost global shipping giant Maersk $300 million and reduced the company to relying on the Facebook-owned WhatsApp messaging system for official corporate communications.

Faced with this scale of loss, some companies want to step up their defenses. Firms with sophisticated technology systems know what's needed to protect their customers, networks and valuable trade secrets. They also likely have employees with the skills to track down hackers and penetrate the attackers' own systems. But the ethics and implications of justifying a cyberattack as defensive get very complicated very quickly.

It's often unclear, for example, exactly who is behind an attack—uncertainty that can last for days, months or even years. So who should the hack-back target? What if a privately owned US company believed that it was under attack from a firm owned by the Chinese government? If it hacked back, would that be an act of war between the countries? What should happen to repair corporate and international relations if the company was wrong and its attacker was somewhere else? Companies shouldn't be empowered to start global cyber conflicts that could have dire consequences, but online and offline.

Of course, it's also important to think about what might happen if other countries allow their companies to hack back against US government or corporate efforts. More US firms could fall victim to cyberattacks as a result, and might find little legal recourse.

Engaging with the Law

At the moment, hacking back is illegal, in the US and in many nations around the world. In the US, the Computer Fraud and Abuse Act makes it a crime to access another computer without authorization. Every member of the G-7, including the US, as well as Thailand and Australia, has banned hacking back. In 2018, more than 50 countries—but not the US—signed an agreement that private firms based in their nations are not allowed to hack back.

However, supporters of active defensive tactics are pushing their message hard. The Republican Party's 2016 presidential platform promised to ensure "users have a self-defense right to deal with hackers as they see fit." In March 2018, the Georgia state legislature passed a bill to permit "active defense measures that are designed to prevent or detect unauthorized computer access." Two months later, then-Gov. Nathan Deal vetoed it, at the urging of technology firms concerned about its "national security implications and other potential ramifications."

Had it become law, Georgia's bill would still likely have run afoul of federal law. However, lawmakers in Washington have also proposed letting companies engage in certain types of active defense. In 2017, US Rep. Tom Graves, a Georgia Republican, proposed the Active Cyber Defense Certainty Act, which would let companies engage in certain active defense measures, including conducting surveillance on prospective attackers, provided that the firm informed the FBI first and that the action did not threaten "public health or safety." The bill died and has not yet been reintroduced; it's not likely to get far in the new Democratic House.

Active defense remains illegal in the US and much of the world. But the bans are not being enforced at home or abroad.

Going Global

Not every country has banned hacking back. Singapore, for example, has been permitting local firms to engage in active defense measures in an effort to prevent, detect, or counter specific threats to its critical infrastructure, including the financial industry.

Other nations, such as France, do not wish to see the private sector out front, but are still keen to keep active defense as an option for governments.

The more countries allow active defense, the more likely everyone—in the US and around the world—is to become a cyberattack victim. Instead of deterring attacks, aggressive active defense increases the possibility of the lights going out, or American voting machines returning inaccurate results.

Organizations can and should be encouraged to take passive defense measures, like gathering intelligence on potential attackers and reporting intrusions. But in my view they should be discouraged—if not prevented—from acting aggressively, because of the risk of destabilizing corporate and international relations. If the quest for cyber peace degenerates into a tit-for-tat battle of digital vigilantism, global insecurity will be greater, not less.

The US Government Uses the Cyberterrorist Threat as an Excuse for Their Hacking

Jeremy Hammond

Jeremy Hammond is a member of the hacktivist network Anonymous and the founder of Hack This Site.

The US has always been the world leader of cyberwar, hacking damn near everyone without any repercussions. And, for years, US intelligence officials and private contractors have been milking hacks to secure billions in cyber security programs: all you need is an enemy, and they will sell you the cure.

Their blatant hypocrisy, threat inflation and militaristic rhetoric must be challenged if we are to have a free and equal internet.

That familiar formula is playing out again with the recent Sony hack. We are supposed to be shocked that these "cyber-terrorists"—purportedly from North Korea—would attack our critical infrastructure and, clearly swift retaliation is in order. But, despite the apocalyptic hype, the Sony hack was not fundamentally different from any other high-profile breach in recent years: personal information was stolen, embarrassing private emails were published and silly political rhetoric and threats were posted on Pastebin. In many ways, it's similar to an Anonymous operation except that, this time, the FBI accused North Korea. That accusation was based on supposed forensic analysis which they have not publicly produced after refusing to participate in joint inquiries.

This official narrative is disputed by many renowned infosec figures. Any skilled hacker or well-financed nation-state practices anti-forensics measures like modifying logs and using proxies to make the attacks appear to originate elsewhere. And North Korea has already been falsely accused of several cyber-attacks—including

"The Government's Cyberterrorism 'Concerns' Are a Pretext for Their Own Hacking Operations," by Jeremy Hammond, Guardian News and Media Limited, February 4, 2015. Reprinted by permission.

attacks against US and South Korean targets in July 2009 and again in 2013. The inherent difficulty of identifying the true attackers should give us pause before we rush to judgment.

It is, however, the perfect pretext for the US to launch their own hacking operations (not that they've ever needed any justification before).

Authorities are once again sounding the cyber-terrorist alarm, promoting a "Free Speech vs North Korea" showdown because the attackers were allegedly angry about *The Interview*, a comedy about a CIA plot to assassinate Kim Jong Un (which Sony reportedly consulted with the State Department and the right-wing RAND Corporation to produce). I am not able to see the movie from prison, so I can't give you a proper critique; maybe it is amusing but, considering the CIA's long and vicious history of assassinations, secret prisons, torture, extrajudicial executions-by-drone and overthrowing democratically-elected governments to install dictatorships, it is not at all surprising Sony would get hacked for making a movie gloating about that.

Sony, too, is an unusual poster child for free-speech advocates in light of their history of lawsuits in defense of their "intellectual property." Years ago, my LulzSec comrades hacked Sony in retaliation for their prosecution of an individual who published information on how to jailbreak the Playstation 3. (Citing the controversial Digital Millennium Copyright Act and the Computer Fraud and Abuse Act, Sony sued not only the original publisher but attempted to go after everyone who even watched the instructional video on YouTube.) This time, Sony's army of lawyers have threatened news organizations and individual Twitter accounts with lawsuits in an atrocious and ultimately ineffective attempt to prevent discussion of their now-public internal emails, demonstrating exactly how they feel about the First Amendment.

When I think about free speech, I am not crying over a multi-billion dollar tech and media empire staging the withdrawal of their movies from theaters to generate PR for a record online release a week later. I'm thinking about the Alien Registration

Act, the Palmer raids, the red scares, the Haymarket Martyrs, COINTELPRO and the House of Unamerican Activities. I think about the harassment of whistleblowers and journalists like Chelsea Manning, Barrett Brown, Julian Assange, James Risen and others, the protesters driven out of public parks at Occupy Wall Street and those that continue to be beaten and arrested at anti-police brutality protests. For seeking the truth, voicing our dissent, and demanding justice, we are criminalized and treated like terrorists.

Invoking the threat of "terrorism" is the biggest smoke-and-mirrors mechanism used to deny citizens both due process and free speech in the 21st century. Law enforcement agents use that word to summon images of 9/11 and Pearl Harbor and stoke public fear into justifying their mass surveillance dragnet—monitoring each and every communication, every internet transaction. The primary targets of these abuses have been Muslims and immigrants, but trumped-up federal terrorism charges have entrapped activists like the Cleveland Five and various earth and animal liberation warriors. Now the latest enemy is "cyber-terrorism": the governments insist that our critical infrastructure is under attack, and we need draconian new measures to protect our "national security."

Sensational Hollywood movies like *Live Free, Die Hard* and the new *Blackhat* propagate this false narrative with ridiculous and unfeasible "terrorist" hacker attacks on nuclear facilities and the power grid. No attacks like this have ever happened, but there is an active effort to recruit independent hackers to sell out and work for the man, purportedly to defend US networks and catch the bad guys.

But when the FBI did arrest a supposed "blackhat"—Hector Monsegur, aka Sabu—and turned him into an informant, they were more interested in hacking targets of their own choosing than preventing attacks on US targets. Despite live knowledge of our ongoing hacking operations through Sabu, they were unable (or unwilling) to stop me from following through with dozens of high profile hacks; some, like the Stratfor breach, they helped facilitate. Instead, Sabu asked me to hack hundreds of foreign government websites from a list he provided, which I regrettably did, unaware of his status as an informant.

And that's what this hype of "cyber-terrorism" is all about: establishing pretexts for our ongoing offensive hacking operations. "...As we implement these responses, some will be seen, others may not be seen," a State Department spokeswoman said as North Korea was hit with repeat cyber-attacks shutting down their internet while more economic sanctions are imposed (through which everyday North Koreans suffer). But for all the accusations against North Korea and China, there is no question that the US has always been the world leader in cyber-warfare. Amongst Snowden's revelations was evidence of the US/Israeli STUXNET, FLAME and DuQu viruses, which infected hundreds of thousands of computers in dozens of countries. They hacked into corporations like Brazil's Petrobas, news agencies like Al Jazeera, DDOS'd Anonymous chat servers, and even tapped the personal cellphones of world leaders. Our unparalleled efforts to assert military-style dominance over the internet is forcing other countries to develop their own hacking units, leading to a digital arms race which makes us all less safe.

If the US truly wanted to stop the proliferation of nation-state hacking, they would push for UN conferences to establish guidelines defining and prohibiting "cyber-warfare." This would require coming clean and putting an end to their own operations, but if they won't even abide by the Geneva Conventions regarding prisoners of war and the use of torture, there's no reason to expect they wouldn't continue hacking in secret. Just as the US government want a monopoly on the use of military force—waging wars to "spread democracy" while condemning those who fight back as "terrorists"—they correspondingly seek a monopoly on the use of hacking. Congress enhances computer crime statutes and the FBI locks up "bad guy" hackers like myself, while recruiting others to work for the government to commit attacks against sovereign countries. Then everyone acts surprised when foreign countries start using the same tactics on us.

When those in power break their own laws then there is no law and no moral authority; there are just competing factions in an international power struggle to control resources like oil, land, drugs and information. Like all wars, only the rich ruling class benefits, and everyone else suffers.

A different kind of cyber-war is possible: not one between nation-states but between the people and their governments. The internet's natural state is anarchy and any attempts to militarize or corporatize it will be owned, exposed and driven offline anyway. I shed no tears when I hear about Sony, CENTCOM or police departments being hacked. In prison, we love hearing about all the bigshots getting hacked by guys like us. So keep on, true-to-the-code blackhats for great justice: instead of selling out your skills to the industry competing for federal contracts supporting US empire, actively undermine it by contributing anti-state solutions by developing encryption, anti-censorship and anonymity infrastructure. We're cheering for you.

The Government Must Not Violate Privacy Rights in the Name of Cybersecurity

Michael O'Neil

Michael O'Neil is a partner at the law firm K & L Gates, where he focuses on international trade, national security, information technology, privacy, and federal policy. He previously served as the North American director of the Trilateral Commission and as counsel for the Central Intelligence Agency (CIA), the Department of Defense, and the US House of Representatives.

Internet regulation—from taxation to censorship—has been a legislative nonstarter in Washington. Yet change the name from regulation to cyber security and one finds an array of legislation that could affect web users in fundamental ways.

Internet security is of much greater concern to the government than to most Americans. Take Internet sabotage. What for many public officials—and some computer security experts as well—is a potentially ominous threat is, for many desk-bound office workers, merely a day's minor excitement. With the advent of each new e-mail-borne virus, firms shut down links to the outside world and wait. Within a few hours everyone is back on line, an anti-virus is in place, and a new cyber war story makes the rounds. Indeed, this pattern of spontaneous disruption has become so commonplace in today's computer-driven businesses that for many of us, it seems an acceptable cost of operating in the digital age.

Yet more than simple complacency is at work here. Popular resistance to greater government involvement in cyber security reflects the same tension that exists in the physical world. Americans certainly could minimize the likelihood of being victimized by robbers if they allowed the local sheriff to camp out in the living room, but for most of us, the resulting loss of privacy wouldn't be worth the marginal increase in security. The same holds true on the Internet. Along with its efficiency, Internet users clearly cherish the anonymity and privacy the new technology affords them. Many users fear that their privacy rights will be diminished if the FBI is out hunting for cyber crooks.

Protecting Critical Infrastructure

Critical infrastructure protection, as posited by the Clinton administration, involves enlisting the private companies that run the nation's energy, transportation, communication, water, and emergency services to help improve the security of the computer systems on which all rely. These services are critical, the theory goes, because they are essential not only to our economy but also to national defense. They can therefore be targeted and, by virtue of their interconnectedness and low security, shut down—by spies, terrorists, hackers, criminals, or even disgruntled employees. Yet this hydra-headed threat hasn't materialized in such a spectacular way as to raise great public alarm and vindicate the government's warnings.

Attacks last February that shut down Yahoo, eBay, and other popular e-commerce sites demonstrated that our computers remain vulnerable and that the possibility of serious economic, if not security, harm does exist. But the only arrest to date suggests that a familiar kind of villain, a teenage computer phenom in his basement, may have been responsible for taking down at least one of the sites. So the threat that government officials worry about, the disabling or destruction of a major service infrastructure, still appears remote. The lack of any enduring damage appears once again to have calmed public fears.

New Technology, Familiar Challenges

The February attacks did get Congress's attention, eliciting several bills in both the House and the Senate to augment law enforcement capabilities to investigate and prosecute computer crime. At the heart of the legislation, and of the administration's plan for infrastructure assurance, is the proposition that the advance of digital communications and information networks has complicated the job of law enforcement—and by corollary that of intelligence agencies as well. But even if that proposition is accepted, privacy concerns will remain, if not grow.

The problem that best makes this case is encryption. No longer the sole province of governments and spies, effective, easy-to-use encryption allows any computer user to communicate and exchange information in a highly secure manner. In an age when vast amounts of personal data are stored in networks—and not at home or in bank vaults—encryption offers privacy protection that is increasingly important to many Americans. Yet their increased personal security may come at a price in apprehending criminals. Criminals and terrorists are now encoding communications and records using the same ubiquitous commercial encryption products. The FBI, the Drug Enforcement Administration, and other law enforcement agencies are hard pressed to break increasingly sophisticated codes used by wrongdoers.

The idea that technological innovations make it harder to catch crooks or spies is not new. The advent of the telephone also forced law enforcement to reexamine its investigative tools. Calls today for expanded cyber crime-fighting authority reveal a great deal about how the government views the challenges to law enforcement in the Digital Age. Sophisticated terrorists might take down the nation's electrical grid, so new security standards are necessary. The nation's telephone system is going digital, so major adjustments must be made to ensure law enforcement's continued ability to wiretap criminals and spies. Denial-of-service attacks against Internet businesses must be prevented, so the scope of existing computer crimes must be expanded to cover damages caused by loss of business.

All these changes can be useful additions to the electronic protections both industry and law enforcement need today. Yet the basis for their justification is also important, because of what it accepts as reasonable and what it will justify in the future. So is it true that technology has increased threats to the American way of life that must be countered by new government surveillance authority? And must government needs and personal privacy expectations be rebalanced?

These questions are hard to answer. Technology is advancing so swiftly that often we cannot perceive how it will affect our lives. In such a climate, it takes genuine prescience or unshakable convictions to know what a proper balance should be. Take, for example, a key weapon in the government's arsenal against computer crime, the Electronic Communications Privacy Act. Enacted in 1986, it governs the protection of, as well as government access to, electronic communications such as e-mail. But in 1986, very few Americans understood the potential of either e-mail or the Internet. The idea that e-mail would greatly displace written and telephone communications between businesses, or even within a business, was entirely foreign. Perhaps as a result, despite the undeniably growing reliance of both businesses and individuals on e-mail, the legal protections afforded e-mail do not match those that apply to either paper records or telephone conversations.

Another government tool whose application to the Digital Age has raised concerns is the pen register, a device used to record the numbers dialed to begin a telephone conversation. Intercepting the actual conversation requires a warrant based on a high evidentiary showing. Obtaining the number dialed requires only the government's certification that the number is relevant to an ongoing criminal investigation. Amendments made in 1986 to the pen register law have been interpreted by the government to extend pen register orders to e-mail messages. Because there is no well-defined parallel between a telephone number and an e-mail address, applying pen register orders to e-mail has raised concerns about the ever-widening scope of government intrusion into Internet communications.

The debate about how to balance government and law enforcement needs with privacy expectations was given a high-voltage jump start in June when it was revealed that the government is using a new Internet sniffing device to monitor web traffic. Called "Carnivore," the device is essentially a stand-alone computer installed at a key node in the system of an Internet service provider. It monitors all traffic carried over the system at that point and selects and stores communications the government is authorized to intercept—sometimes the full text, sometimes only the Internet address. The trouble is that Carnivore is a black box controlled by the government, its programming and selection criteria known only to those who operate it.

Carnivore gives government much more control than Ma Bell ever did. In the predigital age, the government presented its warrant or court order to the telephone company, which in turn routed the specified information to the government listening post. The FBI didn't attach the tap itself, and the common carrier was responsible to the court to ensure that the government got only what the court authorized. Carnivore changes that relationship and with it several independent checks on government action.

The government argues that these shifts in privacy protection are not intentional. It points out that Carnivore is used only by court order and only when an Internet service provider lacks diagnostic and monitoring capabilities to perform the surveillance ordered. Yet in partial recognition of the privacy issues raised by Carnivore, the attorney general recently ordered an independent review by a major university. In the same vein, the Clinton administration has suggested both a "clarification" of the pen register statute's application to the Internet and a requirement that a federal judge weigh the factual basis for a pen register's relevance to a criminal investigation.

The Debate in Congress

These steps are welcome news to personal privacy advocates, but the seriousness of cyber crime and critical infrastructure protection suggests that this debate is just beginning. The Clinton administration and Congress put forth a dizzying range of proposals, including new Internet surveillance provisions, Freedom of Information Act exemptions, regulation of commercial use of consumer information and, inevitably, the creation of a commission to study all the above. Though the 106th Congress did not enact comprehensive legislation affecting Internet privacy, cyber crime, and critical infrastructure protection, the new Congress will address these issues quickly.

What that Congress will take up seems clear enough. Yet unless it is guided by several basic principles, Congress risks addressing them inadequately and without balance.

The first category of issues to be addressed, law enforcement, encompasses two related goals. One reflects a bipartisan consensus to spend money on the problems du jour. In other words, expect Congress to allocate ever more resources for law enforcement to investigate and prosecute hackers and other cyber criminals. The other law enforcement effort likely will strengthen penalties for various computer crimes and expand government authority to police them.

The second category concerns continuing government efforts to get its own house in order. Specifically, look for Congress to fund efforts by federal agencies to better protect their information systems. Most urgent is the shortage of highly trained information technology specialists within the government to protect critical networks, a need just now beginning to be addressed.

Third, Congress undoubtedly will move to protect individuals' privacy rights in the cyber world. In some cases, this step might involve simply applying the same standards from the physical world; in others, it might mean expanding protections to account for the public's growing reliance on electronic communication and record keeping.

Finally, expect Congress to try to create a better climate for information sharing between the government and the private sector, especially concerning threats and attacks on the nation's critical information infrastructure. Bills to accomplish this goal won widespread support in Congress and in industry this year, but fell victim to time.

Principles for Drafting New Laws

How Congress will resolve these matters is critical. Many factors will come into play, ranging from new technological developments to the political makeup of the next Congress and administration. Here are some suggestions as to how Congress, the executive, and the public should think about and work through these important and complex issues.

What is first required is a recognition that technology has changed the nature of individual privacy in fundamental ways. What the founding fathers sought to protect from unreasonable intrusion by the government—the privacy of a citizen's home and personal papers—is no longer found in the home or even on paper. Nowadays, our private information is as likely to be stored on computers, often computers that are part of a network, in electronic files, and often with third parties that many Americans either cannot identify or of whom they are unaware. Communications course through a much more diverse electronic medium than did telephone calls just a dozen years ago. This kind of change is likely to continue—and in ways not easily foreseeable to most of us.

Second, the law, especially federal laws with national scope and application to the government itself, must adjust not only to changes in technology, but to the effect those changes clearly have had on the protection of individual privacy. This task will require dogged perseverance on the part of lawmakers. The law enforcement community will not easily cede surveillance capacity now or in the future. Its battle cry will be preservation, even improvement, of current capability in the face of ever more sophisticated cyber-criminal enterprise. After Congress passed the 1995 Communications Assistance to Law Enforcement Act to require common carriers to modify their equipment to permit government wiretapping of new digital telephone equipment, the industry spent years developing the necessary technical standards, only to have the Justice Department reject them on the grounds that more capabilities could be, and therefore should be, included. When the Federal Communications Commission then largely approved the broad new requirements the Justice Department demanded, a federal appeals court had to point out that the balance between what was technically possible and the protections against unreasonable intrusion had not been struck. Congress had required just such a balancing test in the law, but had not reckoned with the tenacity shown by law enforcement in protecting and expanding its powers.

Third, there will be a great deal to get right the first time among all the issues that are likely to be addressed. For instance, "clarifying" how the pen register law applies to e-mail should make clear whether the subject line is more akin to a telephone number or to message content and to what extent an individual's Internet browsing must be disclosed. A Freedom of Information Act exemption for sharing cyber security information with the government should encourage information sharing not just with law enforcement agencies but between other parts of the government and among private-sector entities. And making computer crime laws tougher should not discourage prosecution, as current juvenile sentencing guidelines do. In the area of commercial privacy protection, a host of issues must be addressed, fleshing out just what notice, disclosure, and consent mean.

Fourth, there is much that neither Congress nor a new administration should try to do. In the area of critical infrastructure protection, cyber security should be improved through voluntary, private-sector-organized mechanisms. This will frustrate some in government, particularly at those times when fresh cyber attacks appear to threaten our use of Internet services. Yet the networks at risk, and the essential service industries they support, are largely designed, built, operated, and maintained by the businesses that own them. To be effective, critical infrastructure protection policy cannot be dictated by government, especially given the government's admitted failure thus far to improve security within its own ranks. Private-sector solutions, not public regulations, are most likely to work best for industry and, ultimately, consumers.

Finally, to return to the point on which I began, the national debate on new cyber law must avoid the dangers of label oversimplification. All the issues discussed above can be grouped together under the rubric of privacy protection. Yet, in the case of cyber crime initiatives, real care will have to be taken to achieve even modest gains in privacy protection. And ensuring effective personal privacy in commercial use of the Internet may well hinge more on better uses of the same software technologies that created the threat in the first place than on new federal laws. Thus, calling what we are doing by its real name—Internet surveillance or increased wiretapping powers in the case of some cyber crime provisions—may be the best way to deal both with the advance of technology and with protecting what remains of our electronic privacy.

Active Self-Defense Is the Future of Cybersecurity

Daniel Lohrmann

Daniel Lohrmann is a cybersecurity expert, technologist, and author. He previously led the Michigan government's cybersecurity and technology infrastructure teams and now serves as the chief security officer (CSO) and chief strategist for Security Mentor, Inc.

All around the world, companies, governments and individuals are becoming increasingly frustrated over the lack of effective solutions to our growing criminal problems in cyberspace. For many, the bad guys are not just winning, they are currently crushing the good guys with few negative consequences.

When it comes to cybercrime, online attacks against critical systems, destructive malware and other forms of cyberattacks, more experts are coming to the conclusion that "just playing defense" is a losing online strategy in the long run.

What can be done? One popular answer is taking the battle to the bad guys. People call it many different things, from offensive cybercapabilities to electronic countermeasures to strikeback to hacking back or hack back.

While there are many different definitions and stories about hacking back, the term basically "involves turning the tables on a cyberhacking assailant: thwarting or stopping the crime, or perhaps even trying to steal back what was taken."

Daniel Lohrmann, "Can 'Hacking Back' Be an Effective Cyber Answer?" February 12, 2016. Published in *Government Technology*. Copyright © 2016 by e.Republic, Inc. All rights reserved. Used with permission.

The Supportive Case for Hacking Back

According to a growing number of security experts, there are steps that could be taken to allow for progress in this area.

In a House Foreign Affairs Committee hearing held in September last year, Chairman Ed Royce, R-Calif., noted that the nation's intelligence chiefs have lamented the lack of a clear national cyberdeterrence strategy:

> "From the private sector to government, our country is taking body blow after body blow in cyberspace," Royce said in his opening statement. "Why aren't we hitting back?"
>
> James Lewis, director and senior fellow in the Center for Strategic and International Studies' Strategic Technologies Program, said hitting back could be just the thing.
>
> "We need to make credible threats," he said. "We need to have countries believe that we will respond with punitive action."
>
> While Israel, Russia and, to a lesser extent, the United Kingdom and France have all shown they'll hit back after a cyberattack, the US has lagged, Lewis said.

Several other experts also testified on what cyber-counter-attack steps might make sense.

But those discussions involved government actions. What about the private sector?

Earlier in 2015, Juan Zarate, the former deputy national security adviser for counterterrorism during President George W. Bush's administration, told a forum at the Hudson Institute that "the US government should deputize private companies to strike back against cyberattackers as a way to discourage widespread threats against the nation's businesses, a former government official says."

> Many US businesses have limited options for defending their IP networks, and the nation needs to develop more "aggressive" capabilities to discourage cyberattacks, said Zarate.
>
> The US government should consider allowing businesses to develop "tailored hack-back capabilities," Zarate said Monday at a forum on economic and cyberespionage hosted by think tank the Hudson Institute. The US government could issue

cyberwarrants, giving a private company license "to protect its system, to go and destroy data that's been stolen or maybe even something more aggressive," he added.

Several panelists at the Hudson event contributed to a new report, *Cyber-Enabled Economic Warfare: An Evolving Challenge.*

Furthermore, the *Guardian* (UK) highlighted the perspectives of Dennis Blair, former director of national intelligence in the Obama administration, who has come out in favor of electronic countermeasures. Here's an excerpt:

> Blair co-authored a 2013 report from the US Commission on the Theft of American Intellectual Property. It considered explicitly authorising strikeback operations but stopped short of endorsing this measure at the time.
>
> Instead, the report suggested exploring non-destructive alternatives, such as electronically tagging stolen data for later detection. It also called for a rethinking of the laws that forbid hacking, even in self-defence.

Significant Concerns with Hacking Back

Beyond the fact that it is illegal to hack back, there are currently a long list of concerns with going on the cyberoffense. Several of these are listed in this Kaspersky blog. Here are four:

- Attackers can remain anonymous forever
- Cyberattacks are asymmetric: a single hacker is capable of successfully destroying an entire company
- It's cheap and easy for hackers to regroup almost anywhere, anytime, even if their systems are physically destroyed
- Organized crime has enthusiastically embraced cybercrime (i.e., don't expect them to play nice)

Along the same lines as item No. 1, researchers point out the difficult problem of attribution—that is knowing who really attacked you in cyberspace.

Jason Hong, associate professor at Central Michigan State University, said, "Companies should absolutely not hack back against cyberthieves. One major concern is attribution, namely knowing that you have identified the right parties. Intruders typically use other people's computers and servers, so odds are high that a company would simply be attacking an innocent party. ..."

Questions abound regarding how this world work if everyone was attacking everyone else, which could lead to even more chaos. What is the threshold test for the level of certainty required to enforce rights?

This *Security Week* article contains quotes from many different industry experts regarding their views on hacking back. I find several of the quotes to be interesting, such as Chris Pogue from Nuix:

> "When asked about the concept of hacking back, the answer is simple. It's cyber vigilantism. It's illegal. Don't do it. So as not to operate in the world of such moral absolutes, let me provide some additional details into why this is a horrible idea:
> 1. Poking the Bear—Attackers, regardless of their skill level, enjoy several advantages, not the least of which is that they are hackers and most IT professionals are not. ...
> 2. Who are you attacking—A large percentage of attacks take place from something called, "Jump Servers" or "Jump Boxes. ..."
> 3. Don't start an international incident—Many countries from which these attacks are launched consider cyber-attacks tantamount to an act of war. ...
> 4. We have people for that—There are federal agencies like the Secret Service, the FBI, the CIA, and the NSA whose job it is to handle situations like this. ..."

Is There Any Middle Ground?

In a *Financial Times* article last summer, John Strand described a set of 20 tricks and traps to thwart cybercriminals.

"The main active defense tactics as the three As: annoyance, attribution and attack. Only two of the three As are considered above-board, however.

Annoyance involves tracking a hacker and leading him into a fake server, wasting his time—and making him easy to detect. A new generation of start-ups is specializing in building traps for data centers, including two Israeli companies, TrapX and Guardicore.

Attribution uses tools to trace the source of an attack back to a specific location, or even an individual hacker. The two most popular tools in the ADHD kit are attribution techniques: the "honey badger," which locates the source of an attack, tracking its latitude and longitude with a satellite picture, and beacons, which are placed in documents to detect when and where data is accessed outside the user's system."

But it is the third A—attack—that is most controversial. To "hack back," a company accesses an alleged hacker's computer to delete its data or even to take revenge. Both of these steps are considered illegal.

I believe that it is important to reiterate the three options laid out by the *Financial Times*: annoyance, attribution and hacking back.

Clarity is important, and there is a big difference between leading a hacker to a fake server (using "honeypots" or other tricks) or trace their sources of attack and taking revenge or deleting data from other systems. No doubt, the lines can get fuzzy at times, but the reality is pretty clear for most people.

Final Thoughts

Despite the many challenges to hacking back that exist today, the concept of self-defense in cyberspace is bound to lead to new laws and new clarity in regard to hacking back.

It seems to me that the biggest difference between a gun self-defense policy and cyber self-defense policy is the absolute certainty that a person has when someone is running at you with a knife or a gun in your home. There is almost no doubt who you are fighting and what needs to be done in the physical world, and cyberspace brings a host of unknowns. Bottom line, attribution is very hard.

Nevertheless, I believe that new approaches will emerge over the coming decade, which may change the playing field in cyberspace. I'm not exactly sure how we will solve the difficulties, but I have a strong feeling that this "hacking back" topic is just beginning to heat up.

CHAPTER 4

Is It Possible to Effectively Combat Cyberterrorism and Other Cyberattacks?

Overview: Technology Is Developing to Help Combat Cyberattacks

Incognito Forensic Foundation

The Incognito Forensic Foundation Lab (IFF Lab) provides digital and cyber forensic solutions for businesses and government agencies. It is based in Bangalore, India.

Are you bummed by the oft-repeated phrase "cybercrimes are getting graver by the day"? Well, unfortunately, it's true. Cybercrime masterminds often have an equivalent technical prowess as their cyber security counterparts! This has led to an ever-evolving landscape of cybercrimes that constantly outsmart modern cyber security technologies. So, does that end our fight against cyber threats? No, the answer lies in increasing cognizance and implementation of advanced cyber security technologies. This blog gives you the 5 latest cyber security technologies that you must be wary of.

Cybercrime Is the New Threat that Terrorizes Nations

In terms of national security, physical terrorism still remains the top concern for nations across the globe. However, the times are changing rapidly, and not for good though! Terrifying as it may sound, the United States has recently declared cyber attacks to be a greater threat to the country than terrorism. And, when one of the most powerful nations in the world expresses such concerns, one can well imagine the vulnerability of small businesses and developing nations to cyber attacks!

In fact, US Homeland Security Chief, Kirstjen Nielsen, believes that the next 9/11 attack is likely to happen online rather than in the physical world. However, it's unfortunate that few governments and public enterprises are still not taking cyber threats as seriously as they should.

The Need to Adopt the Latest Cyber Security Technologies

There's a lot of buzz around cyber attacks in the last couple of years. Does that mean the cybercrimes never existed in the past? Well, they did! Just that the impact was not as severe and large scale. The recent spate of cyber attacks such as WannaCry and NotPetya reaffixed the global attention on the cybercrimes.

Recognizing and deploying advanced cyber security strategies to combat threats is the need of the hour. Here's why one NEEDS to acknowledge cybercrimes, treat them seriously and have preventive measures in place.

1. The Targets of Attack Are Changing

Gone are the days when the targets of cybercrimes would be petty in nature. A cybercrime's prime objective is no longer just vengeance, quick money or extracting confidential details. It has transcended to bigger targets and more sinister motives, more commonly known as cyber warfare. All critical infrastructures, at present, such as utility services, nuclear power plants, healthcare facilities, airports, etc. are connected to a network. By 2030, there would be nearly 30 billion connected devices! So, how many more targets are we creating for cybercrime masterminds to exploit? Mull over it!

2. Cyber Threats Are Becoming More Advanced

Cyber criminals are getting more advanced and sinister by the day. And, don't you think it's that easy to get the better of black-hat hackers! Hackers have the same technical prowess as a top computer science professional. And as technologies to keep cyber threats at bay advance, so do the methods of attack! Skilled blackhat hackers are growing in numbers, and so are sophisticated tools in the dark and deep web.

3. The Aftermath Is Grave

As mentioned earlier, all critical infrastructures are now connected to a worldwide network. In fact, all companies have their business-critical data recorded in digital format and are hence greatly dependent on their systems and networks. In such circumstances, even a small attack on the network or system can have a cascading effect on their operations. Failure to secure such critical networks from potential cyber attacks can endanger credibility, sales, profits, and sometimes, even national security!

4. Critical Shift in the Nature of Cyber Attacks

Imagine what would happen if one manages to hack a power grid or any other public utility infrastructure? Public inconvenience, lost revenues, reputational damage, regulatory penalties, and a whopping expense in restoring operations and improving cyber security measures. The impacts of an attack are no longer restricted to individuals but span across global economic and political systems.

The Top 5 Latest Cyber Security Technologies

Cyber warfare continues to gain heat with newer technologies available to break into systems and networks. There have been many cases of attack on critical infrastructures such as healthcare, water systems, and power grids. On a smaller scale, there has been a spurt in ransomware and malware attacks on enterprise networks.

Man creates technology, and it is the man who can get the better of this technology. Thus, no cyber security mechanism is foolproof and can ever be. The wise choice is to constantly identify and adopt emerging technologies to fortify cyber security. Here's a list of the top advanced cyber security technologies on the charts.

1. Artificial Intelligence & Deep Learning

Artificial Intelligence is quite a buzzword these days. Ever wondered how one can apply AI to cyber security? Well, the application is in a way similar to the working of two-factor authentication.

Two-factor authentication works by confirming a user's identity based on 2-3 different parameters. The parameters being something they know, are and have. Add to that additional layers of information and authentication, and that is where AI comes into the picture. Deep learning is being used to analyze data such as logs, transaction and real-time communications to detect threats or unwarranted activities.

2. Behavioral Analytics

With the whole Facebook Data Breach fray, one is well aware of the use of data mining for behavior analysis. This technique is widely to target social media and online advertisements to the right set of audience. Interestingly, behavior analytics is being increasingly explored to develop advanced cyber security technologies.

Behavioral analytics helps determine patterns on a system and network activities to detect potential and real-time cyber threats. For instance, an abnormal increase in data transmission from a certain user device could indicate a possible cyber security issue. While behavioral analytics is mostly used for networks, its application in systems and user devices has witnessed an upsurge.

3. Embedded Hardware Authentication

A PIN and password are no longer adequate to offer foolproof protection to hardware. Embedded authenticators are emerging technologies to verify a user's identity.

Intel has initiated a major breakthrough in this domain by introducing Sixth-generation vPro Chips. These powerful user authentication chips are embedded into the hardware itself. Designed to revolutionize "authentication security," these employ multiple levels and methods of authentication working in tandem.

4. Blockchain Cybersecurity

Blockchain cyber security is one of the latest cyber security technologies that's gaining momentum and recognition. The blockchain technology works on the basis of identification between the two transaction parties. Similarly, blockchain cyber security works on the basis of blockchain technology's peer-to-peer network fundamentals.

Every member in a blockchain is responsible for verifying the authenticity of the data added. Moreover, blockchains create a near-impenetrable network for hackers and are our best bet at present to safeguard data from a compromise. Therefore, the use of blockchain with Artificial Intelligence can establish a robust verification system to keep potential cyber threats at bay.

5. Zero-Trust Model

As the name itself states, this model of cyber security is based on a consideration that a network is already compromised. By believing that one cannot trust the network, one would obviously have to enhance both "internal" and "external" securities.

The crux here is that both internal and external networks are susceptible to a compromise and need equal protection. It includes identifying business-critical data, mapping the flow of this data, logical and physical segmentation, and policy and control enforcement through automation and constant monitoring.

Blockchain Can Play an Important Role in the Future of Cybersecurity

Nir Kshetri

Nir Kshetri is a professor of management at the University of North Carolina–Greensboro and a research fellow at Kobe University. He is the author of nine books and over 150 articles on blockchain research, and he has provided consulting services to the Asian Development Bank and various UN agencies.

The world is full of connected devices—and more are coming. In 2017, there were an estimated 8.4 billion internet-enabled thermostats, cameras, streetlights and other electronics. By 2020 that number could exceed 20 billion, and by 2030 there could be 500 billion or more. Because they'll all be online all the time, each of those devices—whether a voice-recognition personal assistant or a pay-by-phone parking meter or a temperature sensor deep in an industrial robot—will be vulnerable to a cyberattack and could even be part of one.

Today, many "smart" internet-connected devices are made by large companies with well-known brand names, like Google, Apple, Microsoft and Samsung, which have both the technological systems and the marketing incentive to fix any security problems quickly. But that's not the case in the increasingly crowded world of smaller internet-enabled devices, like light bulbs, doorbells and even packages shipped by UPS. Those devices—and their digital "brains"—are typically made by unknown companies, many in developing countries, without the funds or ability—or the brand-recognition need—to incorporate strong security features.

Insecure "internet of things" devices have already contributed to major cyber-disasters, such as the October 2016 cyberattack

"Using Blockchain to Secure the 'Internet of Things,'" by Nir Kshetri, The Conversation, March 7, 2018. https://theconversation.com/using-blockchain-to-secure-the-internet-of -things-90002. Licensed under CC BY-ND 4.0.

on internet routing company Dyn that took down more than 80 popular websites and stalled internet traffic across the US. The solution to this problem, in my view as a scholar of "internet of things" technology, blockchain systems and cybersecurity, could be a new way of tracking and distributing security software updates using blockchains.

Making Security a Priority

Today's big technology companies work hard to keep users safe, but they have set themselves a daunting task: Thousands of complex software packages running on systems all over the world will invariably have errors that make them vulnerable to hackers. They also have teams of researchers and security analysts who try to identify and fix flaws before they cause problems.

When those teams find out about vulnerabilities (whether from their own or others' work, or from users' reports of malicious activity), they are well positioned to program updates, and to send them out to users. These companies' computers, phones and even many software programs connect periodically to their manufacturers' sites to check for updates, and can download and even install them automatically.

Beyond the staffing needed to track problems and create fixes, that effort requires enormous investment. It requires software to respond to the automated inquiries, storage space for new versions of software, and network bandwidth to send it all out to millions of users quickly. That's how people's iPhones, PlayStations and copies of Microsoft Word all stay fairly seamlessly up to date with security fixes.

None of that is happening with the manufacturers of the next generation of internet devices. Take, for example, Hangzhou Xiongmai Technology, based near Shanghai, China. Xiongmai makes internet-connected cameras and accessories under its brand and sells parts to other vendors.

Many of its products—and those of many other similar companies—contained administrative passwords that were set in the factory and were difficult or impossible to change. That left the door open for hackers to connect to Xiongmai-made devices, enter the preset password, take control of webcams or other devices, and generate enormous amounts of malicious internet traffic.

When the problem—and its global scope—became clear, there was little Xiongmai and other manufacturers could do to update their devices. The ability to prevent future cyberattacks like that depends on creating a way these companies can quickly, easily and cheaply issue software updates to customers when flaws are discovered.

A Potential Answer

Put simply, a blockchain is a transaction-recording computer database that's stored in many different places at once. In a sense, it's like a public bulletin board where people can post notices of transactions. Each post must be accompanied by a digital signature, and can never be changed or deleted.

I'm not the only person suggesting using blockchain systems to improve internet-connected devices' security. In January 2017, a group including US networking giant Cisco, German engineering firm Bosch, Bank of New York Mellon, Chinese electronics maker Foxconn, Dutch cybersecurity company Gemalto and a number of blockchain startup companies formed to develop just such a system.

It would be available for device makers to use in place of creating their own software update infrastructure the way the tech giants have. These smaller companies would have to program their products to check in with a blockchain system periodically to see if there was new software. Then they would securely upload their updates as they developed them. Each device would have a strong cryptographic identity, to ensure the manufacturer is communicating with the right device. As a result, device makers and their customers would know the equipment would efficiently keep its security up to date.

These sorts of systems would have to be easy to program into small devices with limited memory space and processing power.

They would need standard ways to communicate and authenticate updates, to tell official messages from hackers' efforts. Existing blockchains, including Bitcoin SPV and Ethereum Light Client Protocol, look promising. And blockchain innovators will continue to find better ways, making it even easier for billions of "internet of things" devices to check in and update their security automatically.

The Importance of External Pressure

It will not be enough to develop blockchain-based systems that are capable of protecting "internet of things" devices. If the devices' manufacturers don't actually use those systems, everyone's cybersecurity will still be at risk. Companies that make cheap devices with small profit margins won't add these layers of protection without help and support from the outside. They'll need technological assistance and pressure from government regulations and consumer expectations to make the shift from their current practices.

If it's clear their products won't sell unless they're more secure, the unknown "internet of things" manufacturers will step up and make users and the internet as a whole safer.

By Acting Quickly, Hacking Victims Can Reduce the Amount of Damage Done

David Lacey

David Lacey is a senior research fellow in human factors and sociotechnical systems at the University of the Sunshine Coast in Australia. He specializes in identity security and is a director and founder of iDcare, a national identity support service in Australia and New Zealand that was recently launched by the government.

More than at any other point in time, your personal information is worth a lot of money to a lot of people. There's a whole industry created around it that's typically referred to as direct marketing. There's a similar industry also booming in the trade; that's called hacking or data breaching.

Let me explain a slight nuance between the two. The direct marketing industry will typically know more about you than you do. In fact, it knows so much about you, it's willing to sell your details to others so they can better predict your purchasing behaviour before you even get that itch to buy.

It's not confined to those wanting to make a dollar. Government agencies are also on the bandwagon. Agencies want to know where to deliver their services more effectively and where wastage can be cut. The central player in all of this is you. It's just that you are a passive participant. Our data and the identity footprints our personal information creates is what drives these markets.

So what about the criminals? This other market called hacking? Well, they love us too, more specifically our personal information. They too like to make money from selling personal information. But increasingly, those who access personal information illicitly are doing so for ideological reasons.

"The First 72 Hours Are Critical for Hacking Victims," by David Lacey, The Conversation, March 11, 2015. https://theconversation.com/the-first-72-hours-are-critical-for-hacking -victims-37972. Licensed under CC BY-ND 4.0.

Hacking in Vogue

CNet and many other technology commentators described 2014 as "the year of the hack." Leading industry sources such as the United States Identity Theft Resource Center, Gemalto, and Risk Based Security report that between 700 million and 1.1 billion records containing personal information were compromised last year.

A fundamental issue with the volume relates to the grapple with ideology. Hacktivism is not a new concept—Denning wrote about it in 2001 when commenting on the Kosovo crisis of 1998/99.

But hackers don't need Kosovo. All they need is a lack of appropriate controls and a platform to tell the world what they've found to further their political platform.

In October last year the Commonwealth government announced the creation of iDcare. I've a personal and professional interest in such a body, as I'm on its board and see how its operations impact the lives of many each day. It's a joint public and private sector national initiative that operates a toll-free hotline for individuals concerned about their personal information.

In a little over 12 weeks iDcare provided direct assistance to more than 4,000 clients. A fair chunk of these clients were victims of hacking events. What have we learnt in this short amount of time? Hacking of individuals can have dramatic impacts on how they attribute blame, the likelihood of repeat business, and the overall confidence they have in participating online.

Hacking for the most part has little to do with what you or I have done, but what organisations have not done to protect what's ours in their custody. A common way hackers make their point today is by publicly releasing the spoils of their victory—the personal information and communications they have acquired. Some prefer the big bang approach and release their spoils en masse.

Others prefer the more painful drip-fed approach. The recent Aussie Travel Cover hacker went the extra mile to share with the world how they did it—why not educate while inspiring others?

The Protectors

So where does all this leave those of us who represent the information, and those organisations that are the compromised custodians? Like a classical complex system, hacking events, their prevention and response is not a unitary problem for one group or organisation. It's a systems problem, and a complex one at that.

While I'm a proponent of some form of mandatory data breach notification framework, this system is fraught with danger and requires a much deeper consideration of the impacts, their antecedents, associated control failures, and best effort responses.

The first three months of iDcare tells us that the 72 hours following the initial compromise of personal information really counts. In that 72 hours an individual can do things that makes their personal information more resilient to further misuse—you can make your personal information complex and unattractive for the criminal.

Putting credit bans or freezes on your credit file and alerting the right government and business channels that your personal information is at risk are important considerations. These measures can make a misuse more difficult for the hacker and the criminals that purchase such information.

iDcare's data tells us that if nothing is done in the first 72 hours, the chances of a further misuse increases four and a half fold. What does this mean for hacking? It's simple, organisations must prioritise engagement throughout the identity eco-system immediately after a hacking event, least of which is to communicate with impacted individuals, so that they can build resilience to identity theft. The only way to truly understand and effectively respond is to take a systems approach, not solely an organisational one.

A systems approach means organisations examining both the causal nature of hacking, as well the implications of their response across the human, technological and process domains (to name a few).

A response that promotes greater resilience for those individuals that have had their details compromised, has different implications to one that preferences an "ignore it, and it will go away" solution.

There's so much that can go wrong in a response to a hacking event. The Sony Pictures example of 2014-2015 is a great case in point: to release a movie or not; to pay a ransom; to inform current and former employees; to provide assistance to these individuals in order to build their resilience to any further misuse of their identity information; to assist the next of kin of staff who may have also had their details put at risk; to work with law enforcement and national security agencies; to respond to calls from many stakeholders, including even the president of the United States; to respond in a specific way.

How could hacking events be anything but a complex system problem? No wonder the first 72 hours counts. For those organisations that collect and store personal information, better start planning on what your first 72 hours will look like.

Although Challenging, It Is Possible to Attribute Many Cyberattacks

Linda Rosencrance

Linda Rosencrance is a freelance writer and editor in the Boston area. She has written about information technology for more than a dozen years, covering topics such as data loss prevention, network management, mobile application development, big data, analytics, and ERP.

Cyber attribution is the process of tracking, identifying and laying blame on the perpetrator of a cyberattack or other hacking exploit.

Cyberattacks can have serious consequences for businesses in terms of public relations, compliance, reputation and finances. In the wake of an attack, an organization often conducts investigations to attribute the incident to specific threat actors in order to gain a complete picture of the attack, and to help ensure the attackers are brought to justice. These cyber attribution efforts are often conducted in conjunction with official investigations conducted by law enforcement agencies.

Cyber attribution can be very difficult because the underlying architecture of the internet offers numerous ways for attackers to hide their tracks.

Challenges of Cyber Attribution

Companies often lack the resources or expertise needed to track down cybercriminals, so organizations that need to do cyber attribution usually hire outside information security experts. However, cyber attribution can be challenging, even for cybersecurity experts.

"Cyber Attribution," by Linda Rosencrance, TechTarget, October 2017. Reprinted by permission.

To determine the actor or actors responsible for a cyberattack, experts often conduct extensive forensic investigations, including analyzing digital forensic evidence and historical data, establishing intent or motives, and taking into account the overarching situation.

However, one of the challenges of cyber attribution is that hackers don't typically carry out attacks from their own homes or places of business, but launch cyberattacks using computers or devices owned by other victims that the attacker has previously compromised.

Identifying an attacker is also made more difficult because attackers can spoof their own IP addresses or use other techniques, such as proxy servers, to bounce their IP addresses around the world to confuse attempts at cyber attribution.

Additionally, jurisdictional limitations can hinder attribution in cross-border cybercrime investigations because every time a law enforcement agency has to undertake an investigation that crosses borders, it must go through official channels to request help. This can hamper the process of gathering evidence, which must be collected as soon as possible.

In some cases, cyber attribution efforts are further hampered when attacks originate in nations that refuse to cooperate with US law enforcement investigations. Jurisdictional issues can also affect the integrity of the evidence and the chain of custody.

Cyber Attribution Techniques

Cybercrime investigators have many different, specialized techniques available for performing cyber attribution, but definitive and accurate cyber attribution is not always possible.

Investigators use analysis tools, scripts and programs to uncover critical information about attacks. Cybercrime investigators are often able to uncover information about the programming language and related information, including the compiler used, compile time, libraries used and order of the execution of events related to a cyberattack. For example, if investigators can determine a piece of malware was written using a Chinese, Russian or some other language keyboard layout, that information can help narrow down suspects for cyber attribution.

Investigators attempting to do cyber attribution also analyze any metadata connected to the attack. The metadata, including source IP addresses, email data, hosting platforms, domain names, domain name registration information and data from third-party sources can help make the case for attribution because systems used for cyberattacks often communicate with nodes outside the network being targeted. However, these data points can also be easily faked.

Investigators may also analyze metadata collected from multiple attacks targeting different organizations. Doing so enables experts to make some assumptions and assertions based on the recurrence of falsified data they identify. For example, security professionals may be able to trace an anonymous email address from an attack and link it back to the attacker based on domain names used in the attack that were previously identified as being used by a specific threat actor.

Another approach for investigators is to examine the techniques, procedures and tactics used in an attack, because cyberattackers often have their own distinctive and recognizable styles. Investigators are sometimes able to identify perpetrators based on clues related to attack methods, such as social engineering tactics or reuse of malware used in prior attacks.

Knowing what's happening within certain industries or certain companies can also help cybercrime investigators predict attacks. For instance, companies in the natural gas industry spend more money on exploration when gas prices increase and, consequently, are at a higher risk for theft of geospatial data.

Understanding the attacker's motives can also aid in cyber attribution. Security experts work to understand the perpetrators' objectives, because it's not always about money. Investigators aim to figure out if the cybercriminals are just lurking or if they've been spying for a long time. They also try to discover whether the hackers are looking for specific data during their attacks, and how they try to use what they find.

Although cyber attribution isn't an exact science, these attribution techniques can help cybercrime investigators identify the attackers beyond a reasonable doubt.

Online Attribution Is Sometimes Impossible Due to a Wide Range of Obstacles

Cynthia Brumfield

Cynthia Brumfield is a communications and technology analyst who is currently focused on cybersecurity. She runs a cybersecurity news destination site, Metacurity.com.

Attributing cyberattacks to a particular threat actor is challenging, particularly an intricate attack that stems from a nation-state actor, because attackers are good at hiding or erasing their tracks or deflecting the blame to others.

The best method for arriving at a solid attribution is to examine the infrastructure and techniques used in the attack, but even then, researchers can often get it wrong, as Paul Rascagneres and Vitor Ventura of Cisco Talos illustrated in a talk at the VB2020 conference on September 30.

Researchers typically rely on three sources of intelligence, Rascagneres said: open-source intelligence (OSINT), which is publicly available information on the internet, technical intelligence (TECHINT) that relies on malware analysis, and proprietary data available only to the organizations involved in the incident.

Nation-state intelligence agencies serve as another source of intelligence because they have more information and additional resources than the private sector, but intel agencies are often secretive about their methods. "In public sectors, they don't give everything," Rascagneres said. "They don't explain how they get all the detail. How does it make the link?"

Attributing WellMess Malware

Rascagneres walked through an example of analyzing infrastructure and how that can mislead a security researcher. He presented

"Common Pitfalls in Attributing Cyberattacks," by Cynthia Brumfield, CSO, October 16, 2020. Reprinted by permission.

the example in terms of what security investigators call tactics, techniques and procedures (TTP). He focused on the case of multiplatform malware named WellMess discovered by the Japanese national CERT in 2018.

The UK's National Cyber Security Centre (NCSC) directly attributed the WellMess malware to APT29, a Russian state-backed threat group better known as Cozy Bear. That assessment was endorsed by Canada's Communications Security Establishment (CSE), the US's National Security Agency (NSA), and Department of Homeland Security's Cybersecurity and Infrastructure Security Agency (CISA).

WellMess, which extracts information from infected hosts while awaiting further instruction, has 32-bit and 64-bit variants and has multiple protocols to conduct C2 communications including DNS, HTTP and HTTPS. By looking at the infrastructure, researchers can deduce connections between malware samples. For example, if malware A uses infrastructure X and malware B associated with a threat actor M also uses infrastructure X, the attacks are linked through the shared infrastructure.

This technique can be used to investigate shared IP addresses and domains because a lot of different customers can use the same IP addresses. "Based on the IP only, it's a bit tricky and you can easily make a mistake," Rascagneres said.

"The other important thing is the time lapse. The IP address can change quickly from customer to customer. If you have a threat actor that uses a specific IP address on this date and you see another campaign one year later, you have a lot of change at the IP and it's not linked."

Based on an analysis of the IP addresses, WellMess appeared to be malware that originated with APT28, also known as Fancy Bear, not APT29, an attribution that would run counter to what the UK authorities found. Even using TPP, the attribution analysis could lead researchers to the wrong threat group.

Using another WellMess sample, Rascagneres examined the TPP and found a connection between WellMess and the DarkHotel attack group when running the sample through VirusTotal. The DarkHotel group is believed to operate out of the Korean peninsula and steals valuable data from high-level targets such as CEOs. The group's name is derived from DarkHotel's method of tracking travelers' plans and compromising them via hotel Wi-Fi.

Further complicating an analysis of this sample was a report by Chinese security company CoreSec360 that WellMess was an entirely unknown actor they named APT-C-42. But, despite using the three sources of intelligence available to private sector parties, the attribution analysis was unable to reach the conclusion obtained by the NCSC that the attackers were APT29.

Analyzing Shared Code

Analyzing shared code is another commonly used techniques in the attribution process. "We do it because we can see that this sample belongs to that sample and then later down the road" the second sample might be linked to a country or to a group, Ventura said. "Then because of that we are able to do the jump forward to the attribution."

However, Ventura warns would-be attribution researchers that the opposite can be true, particularly when the shared code is publicly available. In those cases, the code similarities can lead to wrong attribution. One researcher Ventura knows tied together two malware samples because of shared code. Later, however, it turned out the code was actually part of an embedded TLS library, a public source widely used by developers and unlikely to provide reliable strong links between two malware samples. "In this case, we have all the overlaps but when we do the further research, when we look into the rest of the information that we have available, we actually disprove our theory."

Beware False Flags

False flags might also lead researchers to a wrong conclusion, Ventura said. The most recent high-profile public example of a false flag is the Olympic Destroyer malware that hit the PyeongChang

Olympics in South Korea in 2018. Security experts who examined the malware attributed it variously to Russia, Iran, China and North Korea due to the false flags embedded in the malware to confuse researchers.

When it comes to false flags, this is where the intelligence agencies "have the upper hand," Ventura said. "They have information that we don't have. They have SIGINT [signals intelligence], they have human intelligence. They have all kinds of information that typically we don't have. We don't have a lot of information."

Ventura touched upon what may be a source of frustration for security researchers, the inability to ever know why intelligence agencies make their attributions. "For us researchers, that makes us extremely uncomfortable because we like verifiable things. I cannot verify it because we just don't have the information."

The best coping mechanism in this case is to simply accept that some things may never be known. "That's a point that we need to accept," Ventura said. "Not that we should accept all that they say as set in stone, but we need to accept that they might not be able to share that information."

Cyberattack Tools Are More Widely Available Than Ever and Can Take Down High-Profile Targets

Nir Kshetri

Nir Kshetri is a professor of management at the University of North Carolina–Greensboro and a research fellow at Kobe University. He is the author of nine books and over 150 articles on blockchain research, and he has provided consulting services to the Asian Development Bank and various UN agencies.

It is looking increasingly likely that computer hackers have in fact successfully attacked what had been the pinnacle of cybersecurity—the US National Security Agency (NSA). A few days ago, reports began emerging of claims by a hacking group called the Shadow Brokers that it had breached the network of, and accessed critical digital content from, computers used by the Equation Group. This attracted more than the usual amount of attention because the Equation Group is widely believed to be a spying element of the NSA.

It is possible—perhaps even likely—that Shadow Brokers is a group of hackers linked to the Russian government.

Shadow Brokers posted online some examples of the data it said it had stolen, including scripts and instructions for breaking through firewall protection. Cybersecurity analysts poring over that information are confident that the material is in fact from Equation Group. This news raises a bigger question: What are the consequences if the Equation Group—and by extension the NSA—were actually hacked?

"After the NSA Hack: Cybersecurity in an Even More Vulnerable World," by Nir Kshetri, The Conversation, August 19, 2016. https://theconversation.com/after-the-nsa-hack -cybersecurity-in-an-even-more-vulnerable-world-64090. Licensed under CC BY-ND 4.0.

What Has Been Breached?

The NSA holds a massive amount of data, including information on US citizens' and foreign nationals' phone calls, social connections, emails, web-browsing sessions, online searches and other communications. How much data? NSA's Utah data center alone is reported to have a storage capacity of 5 zetabytes—1 trillion gigabytes. However, judging from what has been made public of what has been stolen by Shadow Brokers, this massive data trove has not been breached.

But the NSA's other key digital asset is a collection of very sophisticated, often custom-designed, hacking analysis and surveillance software. The agency uses these tools to break into computer networks at home and abroad to spy on specific targets and the public at large.

The Shadow Brokers have claimed to have copies of this software and information on security vulnerabilities the NSA uses in its attacks, including instructions for breaking into computer networks. If true, these would be of very high strategic value to someone seeking to defend against cyberattacks, or wanting to conduct their own.

What Is the Equation Group?

The Equation Group has been closely watched since its existence was first revealed in an early 2015 report by security researchers at Kaspersky Lab, a Russian-based computer security company. Cyberattacks using the Equation Group's signature methods have been carried out since 2001, using extremely specific customized techniques.

In addition to engineering the attacks to ensure a very low risk of detection, they maintain a close watch on their targets to ensure their surveillance does in fact go undetected. And the number of targets they choose is very small—tens of thousands of computers as opposed to the hundreds of thousands or even tens of millions of machines hacked in other major attacks.

Equation Group's targets included government and diplomatic institutions, companies in diverse sectors as well as individuals in more than 30 countries.

Kaspersky Lab reports that China and Russia are among the countries most infected by the Equation Group's hacking tools. Among the alleged targets were the Russian natural gas company Gazprom and the airline Aeroflot. Likewise, China's major mobile companies and universities were allegedly victimized by the NSA.

Who Hacks Whom?

Cyberweapons and their capabilities are becoming an increasing part of international relations, forming part of foreign policy decisions and even sparking what has been called a "cyber arms race."

The Shadow Brokers attack may be a part of this global interplay. The US government is considering economic sanctions against Russia, in response to the alleged cyberattack on the Democratic National Committee computers by two Russian intelligence agencies. Those same attackers are believed to have been behind the 2015 cyberattacks on the White House, the State Department and the Joint Chiefs of Staff.

If the material Shadow Brokers have stolen can link cyberattacks on Gazprom, Aeroflot and other Russian targets with the NSA, Russia can argue to the international community that the US is not an innocent victim, as it claims to be. That could weaken support for its sanctions proposal.

Russia and China, among other adversaries, have used similar evidence in this way in the past. Edward Snowden's revelation of the US PRISM surveillance program, monitoring vast amounts of internet traffic, became an important turning point in China-US cyberrelations. Commenting on the NSA's alleged hacking of China's major mobile companies and universities, an editorial in China's state-run Xinhua News Agency noted: "These, along with previous allegations, are clearly troubling signs. They demonstrate that the United States, which has long been trying to play innocent as a victim of cyberattacks, has turned out to be the biggest villain in our age."

In general, allegations and counterallegations have been persistent themes in Chinese-American interactions about cybercrimes and cybersecurity. China's approach shifted toward more offensive strategies following Snowden's revelation of the PRISM surveillance program. It is likely that this hack of cyberweapons may provide China and other US adversaries with even more solid evidence to prove American involvement in cyberattacks against foreign targets.

Cyberattack Tools Now More Widely Available

There are other dangers too. Hackers now have access to extremely sophisticated tools and information to launch cyberattacks against military, political and economic targets worldwide. The NSA hack thus may lead to further insecurity of cyberspace.

The attack is also further proof of the cybersecurity industry's axiom about the highly asymmetric probabilities of successful attack and successful defense: Attackers need to succeed only once; defenders have to be perfect every time. As sophisticated as NSA's highly secure network is, the agency cannot ever fully protect itself from cyberattackers. Either these attackers have already gotten in, or some other group will be the first to do so in the future.

Actors with fewer financial and technical resources can compromise high-value targets. What will come of this attack remains to be seen, but the potential for profound and wide-ranging, even global, effects is clear.

Organizations to Contact

The editors have compiled the following list of organizations concerned with the issues debated in this book. The descriptions are derived from materials provided by the organizations. All have publications or information available for interested readers. This list was compiled on the date of publication of the present volume; the information provided here may change. Be aware that many organizations take several weeks or longer to respond to inquiries, so allow as much time as possible.

Center for Internet Security (CIS)

31 Tech Valley Drive #2
East Greenbush, NY 12061
(518) 266-3460
website: www.cisecurity.org

The Center for Internet Security (CIS) is a nonprofit organization that was founded in 2000 with the goal of identifying, developing, and supporting best practices in cyber defense. The organization operates on a closed crowdsourcing model and its members include government agencies, academic institutions, and major corporations. It publishes CIS Benchmarks and CIS Controls, which are internationally recognized best practice guidelines for IT and data security. It also hosts the Multi-State Information Sharing and Analysis Center (MS-ISAC).

CyberNB

40 Crowther Lane, Suite 220
Fredericton, New Brunswick
E3C 0J1
Canada
(506) 453-5628
email: info@cybernb.ca
website: www.cybernb.ca

CyberNB is a Canadian nonprofit organization that was founded in 2016 and partners with collaborators in government, academia, and business to fill crucial gaps in Canada's cybersecurity. It focuses on four core areas: ensuring that businesses comply with data security best practices to maintain consumer trust, innovating cybersecurity infrastructure to address digital threats, promoting proper education and training for future cybersecurity talent, and helping cybersecurity companies grow.

801 Labs

353 East 200 South, Suite B
Salt Lake City, UT 84111
(801) 828-3183
email: board@801labs.org
website: www.801labs.org

Based in Salt Lake City, 801 Labs is a nonprofit organization and hackerspace that was created by local information technology, information security, and electronics enthusiasts to establish a hacker community. One of its primary focuses is developing information security. Its physical space serves as a center for peer learning and knowledge sharing, which it facilitates by hosting lectures, workshops, and presentations. Events are open to the public and mostly free, and they can often be accessed electronically through the organization's Discord, Slack, and YouTube channels.

Electronic Frontier Foundation (EFF)

815 Eddy Street
San Francisco, CA 94109
(415) 436-9333
email: info@eff.org
website: www.eff.org

The Electronic Frontier Foundation (EFF) is a nonprofit organization that defends civil liberties in the digital world. It was founded in 1990 and uses grassroots activism, litigation, policy analysis, and technological innovation to protect free expression and user privacy on the internet. It has taken on numerous legal cases against the US government and private companies such as Sony to defend internet users from unlawful surveillance and censorship, which are outlined on its website. It is currently operating campaigns to discourage invasive digital surveillance at local and national levels and to encourage Congress to support litigation that protects strong encryption.

Federal Bureau of Investigation (FBI)

FBI Headquarters
935 Pennsylvania Avenue NW
Washington, DC 20535-0001
(202) 324-3000
website: www.fbi.gov

The Federal Bureau of Investigation is the US government's principal federal law enforcement agency and its domestic intelligence and security service. Some of its main priorities include protecting the US from terrorist attacks, neutralizing cybercrime threats, running counterintelligence programs—many of which are cyber-based. It includes 30,000 agents and partners with government agencies and the private sector to promote national security.

Kaspersky Lab
500 Unicorn Park Drive, #300
Woburn, MA 01801
(866) 328-5700
email: info@kaspersky.com
website: usa.kaspersky.com

Kaspersky Lab is a Russian multinational cybersecurity provider headquartered in Moscow, Russia. It was founded in 1997 and develops antivirus, internet security, and other cybersecurity software. The Kaspersky Global Research and Analysis Team (GReAT) has conducted research that uncovered sophisticated cyber-espionage campaigns by various countries. It also publishes the *Global IT Security Risks Survey* each year.

National Counterterrorism Center (NCTC)
Washington, DC 20511
(703) 275-3700
email: dni-media@dni.gov
website: www.dni.gov/index.php/nctc-home

The National Counterterrorism Center (NCTC) is a US government organization that is responsible for national and international counterterrorism efforts. It advises the US government on issues related to counterterrorism and is part of the Office of the Director of National Intelligence (ODNI). It was established in 2003 as a response to the September 11, 2001, terrorist attacks. Promoting cybersecurity is one of the organization's primary goals, and its website provides reports on cybersecurity as well as tip sheets for individuals on how to promote cybersecurity.

National CyberWatch Center

Prince George's Community College
Center for Advanced Technology, Room 129C
301 Largo Road
Largo, MD 20774
email: info@ncc.flywheelsites.com
website: www.nationalcyberwatch.org

The National CyberWatch Center is a consortium of government agencies, businesses, and higher education institutions that focuses on advancing information security. It aims to help develop, promote, and provide cybersecurity education on a national level. It offers resources for cybersecurity students including educational and training resources, webcasts, and information about internship and employment opportunities. It develops cybersecurity curricula for degree and certification issues that respond to current issues in cybersecurity, hosts academic conferences and collegiate competitions on cybersecurity, and publishes *Cybersecurity Skills Journal: Practice and Research.*

Office of the Director of National Intelligence (ODNI)

Washington, DC 20511
(703) 733-8600
email: dni-media@dni.gov
website: www.dni.gov

The director of national intelligence (DNI) is a cabinet-level official of the US government who acts as the head of the US Intelligence Community (IC), which is composed of eighteen intelligence agencies and organizations that engage in various intelligence activities to promote US national security and foreign policy. The Office of the Director of National Intelligence (ODNI) oversees these activities and synchronizes intelligence collection, analysis, and counterintelligence across the IC. The ODNI website contains a library of its directives and reports.

Privacy International (PI)
62 Britton Street
London, EC1M 5UY
UK
email: info@privacyinternational.org
website: www.privacyinternational.org

Privacy International (PI) is a UK-based charity organization that was formed in 1990 with the intention of defending and promoting the right to privacy around the world. It partners with civil society organizations in numerous countries to raise awareness of privacy issues and help defend them. It investigates privacy violations and campaigns against invasive practices by private corporations and governments. Today, most of its campaigns focus on the intersection of privacy rights and technology, including communications surveillance, data retention, and human rights violations made in the name of counterterrorism.

United Nations Office of Counter-Terrorism (UNOCT)
Department of Global Communications
United Nations Headquarters
405 East 42nd Street
New York, NY 10017
(212) 963-1234
email: education-outreach@un.org
website: www.un.org/counterterrorism

The United Nations Office of Counter-Terrorism (UNOCT) was adopted by the UN General Assembly on June 15, 2017. Its purpose is to provide leadership on counterterrorism mandates by the General Assembly, promote coherence across the Global Counter-Terrorism Coordination Compact entities, strengthen counterterrorism assistance to member states, improve visibility of the UN's counterterrorism efforts, and prevent terrorist and violent extremist attacks on the UN and its member states. Promoting cybersecurity is one of UNOCT's goals, and it has several initiatives to advance cybersecurity.

Bibliography

Books

Babak Akhgar and Ben Brewster, eds. *Combatting Cybercrime and Cyberterrorism: Challenges, Trends and Priorities* (Advanced Sciences and Technologies for Security Applications*). New York, NY: Springer, 2016.

Julian Assange, Jacob Appelbaum, Jérémie Zimmermann, and Andy Muller-Maguhn. *Cypherpunks: Freedom and the Future of the Internet.* New York, NY: OR Books, 2016.

Imran Awan and Brian Blakemore, eds. *Policing Cyber Hate, Cyber Threats and Cyber Terrorism.* London, UK: Routledge, 2016.

Ben Buchanan. *The Hacker and the State: Cyber Attacks and the New Normal of Geopolitics.* Cambridge, MA: Harvard University Press, 2020.

Thomas M. Chen and Strategic Studies Institute. *Cyberterrorism After Stuxnet.* Carlisle Barracks, PA: United States Army War College Press, 2014.

Elizabeth Van Wie Davis. *Shadow Warfare: Cyberwar Policy in the United States, Russia, and China.* London, UK: Rowman & Littlefield, 2021.

Laura DeNardis. *The Internet in Everything: Freedom and Security in a World with No Off Switch.* New Haven, CT: Yale University Press, 2020.

Eamon Doyle, ed. *The Dark Web* (Current Controversies). New York, NY: Greenhaven Publishing, 2019.

Michael Hayden. *Playing to the Edge: American Intelligence in the Age of Terror.* New York, NY: Penguin Press, 2016.

John G. Horgan. *The Psychology of Terrorism* (Political Violence). 2nd ed. London, UK: Routledge, 2014.

Fred Kaplan. *Dark Territory: The Secret History of Cyber War.* New York, NY: Simon & Schuster, 2017.

Megan Manzano, ed. *Cyberwarfare* (At Issue). New York, NY: Greenhaven Publishing, 2018.

Erin L. McCoy. *Cyberterrorism.* New York, NY: Cavendish Square Publishing, 2019.

Michael Miller. *Cyberspies: Inside the World of Hacking, Online Privacy, and Cyberterrorism.* Minneapolis, MN: Twenty-First Century Books, 2021.

Malcolm W. Nance, Chris Sampson, and Ali H. Soufan. *Hacking ISIS: How to Destroy the Cyber Jihad.* New York, NY: Skyhorse Publishing, 2018.

Alison Lawlor Russell. *Cyber Blockades.* Washington, DC: Georgetown University Press, 2014.

David E. Sanger. *The Perfect Weapon: War, Sabotage, and Fear in the Cyber Age.* New York, NY: Crown Publishing Group, 2018.

Peter W. Singer and Allan Friedman. *Cybersecurity: What Everyone Needs to Know.* New York, NY: Oxford University Press, 2014.

Robert E. Taylor, Eric J. Fritsch, and John Liederbach. *Digital Crime and Digital Terrorism.* 3rd ed. New York, NY: Pearson, 2019.

Gary Wiener, ed. *Cyberterrorism and Ransomware Attacks* (Global Viewpoints). New York, NY: Greenhaven Publishing, 2018.

Kim Zetter. *Countdown to Zero Day: Stuxnet and the Launch of the World's First Digital Weapon.* New York, NY: Crown Publishing Group, 2015.

Periodicals and Internet Sources

Frank Bajak, "How the Kremlin Provides a Safe Harbor for Ransomware," ABC News, April 16, 2021. https://abcnews .go.com/Politics/wireStory/kremlin-safe-harbor -ransomware-77111472.

Brian Barrett, "Alleged Russian Hacker Behind $100 Million Evil Corp Indicted," *Wired*, December 5, 2019. https://www .wired.com/story/alleged-russian-hacker-evil-corp- indicted/.

Katie Benner and Nicole Periroth, "China-Backed Hackers Broke into 100 Firms and Agencies, US Says," *New York Times*, September 16, 2020. https://www.nytimes .com/2020/09/16/us/politics/china-hackers .html?searchResultPosition=3.

Megan Brenan, "Cyberterrorism Tops List of 11 Potential Threats to US," Gallup, March 22, 2021. https://news.gallup .com/poll/339974/cyberterrorism-tops-list-potential -threats.aspx.

Doina Chiacu, "White House Warns Companies to Step Up Cybersecurity: 'We Can't Do It Alone.'" Reuters, June 3, 2021. https://www.reuters.com/technology/white-house -warns-companies-step-up-cybersecurity-2021-06-03/.

Jon Gambrell, "Iran Calls Natanz Atomic Site Blackout 'Nuclear Terrorism,'" Associated Press, April 11, 2021. https://apnews .com/article/middle-east-iran-358384f03b1ef6b65f4264bf9 a59a458.

Kathy Gilsinan, "If Terrorists Launch a Major Cyberattack, We Won't See It Coming," *Atlantic*, November 1, 2018. https:// www.theatlantic.com/international/archive/2018/11 /terrorist-cyberattack-midterm-elections/574504/.

Michael L. Gross, Daphna Canetti, and Dana R. Vashdi, "Cyberterrorism: Its Effects on Psychological Well-Being, Public Confidence and Political Attitudes," *Journal of*

Cybersecurity, February 15, 2017. https://academic.oup
.com/cybersecurity/article/3/1/49/2999135.

Sue Halpern, "Should the US Expect an Iranian Cyberattack?"
New Yorker, January 6, 2020. https://www.newyorker
.com/tech/annals-of-technology/should-the-us-expect
-an-iranian-cyberattack.

Clifford Krauss, "Hackers and Climate Change Threaten US
Energy Independence," *New York Times*, May 19, 2021.
https://www.nytimes.com/2021/05/18/business/energy
-environment/colonial-pipeline-security-weather.html.

Karlin Lillington, "How Real Is the Threat of Cyberterrorism?"
Irish Times, April 14, 2016. https://www.irishtimes
.com/business/technology/how-real-is-the-threat-of
-cyberterrorism-1.2608935.

Joseph Moreno and Samuel Curry, "Why America Must Take
the Fight Against Cyberterrorism Seriously," *The Hill*, July 9,
2019. https://thehill.com/opinion/national-security/452172
-why-america-must-take-the-fight-against-cyberterrorism
-seriously.

Ellen Nakashima, "US Accuses Hacker of Stealing Military
Members' Data and Giving It to ISIS," *Washington Post*,
October 16, 2015. https://www.washingtonpost.com/world
/national-security/in-a-first-us-charges-a-suspect-with
-terrorism-and-hacking/2015/10/15/463447a8-738b-11e5
-8248-98e0f5a2e830_story.html.

Nicholas Schmidle, "The Digital Vigilantes Who Hack Back,"
New Yorker, April 30, 2018. https://www.newyorker
.com/magazine/2018/05/07/the-digital-vigilantes-who
-hack-back.

Terry Thompson, "The Colonial Pipeline Ransomware Attack
and the SolarWinds Hack Were All but Inevitable—Why
National Cyber Defense Is a 'Wicked' Problem," *The
Conversation*, May 10, 2021. https://theconversation

.com/the-colonial-pipeline-ransomware-attack-and-the
-solarwinds-hack-were-all-but-inevitable-why-national
-cyber-defense-is-a-wicked-problem-160661.

Jacqueline Thomson, "Cyberattacks Are a Constant Fear 17
Years After 9/11," *The Hill*, September 11, 2018. https://
thehill.com/policy/cybersecurity/405978-cyberattacks-are
-a-constant-fear-17-years-after-9-11.

John Turley, "Why the White House Won't Define Pipeline
Attack as Terrorism," *The Hill*, May 15, 2021. https://thehill
.com/opinion/white-house/553690-why-the-white-house
-wont-define-darksides-pipeline-attack-as-terrorism.

Index